YOU TURN ME ON,

I'M A RADIO

YOU TURN ME ON,

I'M A RADIO

MY WILD ROCK 'N' ROLL LIFE

By ANITA GEVINSON

For
Kathy,
Any friend of Fran's....
Thanks for taking
this journey with
me. Keep
Rockin',
Love,
Aretta
xoxo

3

Note to readers:

This work is a memoir. It reflects the author's present recollection of her experiences over a period of years. Certain names and identifying characteristics have been changed. Dialogue and events have been recreated from memory, and, in some cases, have been compressed to convey the substance of what was said or what occurred. Some scenes are composites of events, and the timeline for some events has been compressed.

For my listeners.

Thank you for tuning in and making my life so

amazing.

CONTENTS

INTRODUCTION

In the eighties my life looked like a perfect rock 'n' roll video that would play over and over on MTV. I was a wildly popular DJ on Philadelphia's top radio station. I was—and still am—the only woman to host a rock 'n' roll morning show in a major radio market. My picture, featuring three-foot cleavage, was on billboards in three states. I was paid a lot of money to play rock music and host a nonstop party with a guest list that included Van Halen, the Pretenders, and Stevie Nicks. I rubbed more than elbows with Daryl Hall, Bob Weir, Carl Palmer, Marty Balin, Billy Squier, and Nils Lofgren.

Just when I thought my life couldn't get any better, Bruce Springsteen or Jackson Browne would show up. And I had a life-changing encounter with

Bob Dylan. In 1983, the love of my life, Warren Zevon, asked me to marry him. So how the fuck did we end up in rehab? And why did I get fired, and replaced with Howard Stern?

Turn up your favorite music, roll up a fat one, or do whatever you need to do to relax, and I'll tell you all about it.

1

My career in radio didn't begin in the usual way. I never had to "pay my dues" or work the overnight shift at a small town radio station for no money. I started large. October 17, 1976 was my first day on the radio at WCAU-FM, a R&B station in Philadelphia. I was hired to host a weekly five-hour show on Sunday mornings from 9 A.M. until 2 P.M. I followed a medical call-in show hosted by married doctors named "The Bricklins". Their show aired once a week as part of required public service programming.

WCAU-FM was an odd fit for a twenty-four-year-old white Jewish rock 'n' roll freak, but it was great training. I attended a Philadelphia broadcasting school every Saturday afternoon for six whole weeks, but I still didn't know how to play a record on a turntable. Luckily WCAU-FM was one of the first automated stations. All the music was pre-scheduled by the program and music directors. The songs were then recorded on those square plastic eight-track cartridges. About twenty minutes before showtime, I went to the computer room to print a list of the songs I would play for the next five hours. The titles were numbered so all I had to do was match the song with the eight-track cart, load them into a giant machine, and then I could "fuhgeddaboudit".

Once the Bricklins left the studio I took a seat in front of a small monitor that had the names and lengths of all the songs that I would play. There was even a number that indicated how many seconds you could talk over the music until the vocal would start. When I saw the letters V.T. (for "voice track") appear on the screen it was my turn to speak. If for some reason I couldn't talk, three seconds later the next song or commercial would automatically start. It was perfectly "foolproof" but also nerve-wracking. When my initial song started to end, I turned the microphone button on and off about twenty times before I had the courage to speak. My first words on-air were "That's Natalie Cole and 'Mr. Melody' on 'Fascinatin' Rhythm FM 98. . . I'm Anita, and here's the latest from Harold Melvin and the Bluenotes, 'Baby, You Got My Nose Open' on FM 98!" I turned off the microphone and exhaled. It was the most amazing feeling in the world and I couldn't believe it was really happening.

Since I didn't have to choose which songs to play, I didn't have much to do. There was lots of downtime to scribble what I was going to say next. I also had time to answer the phones while the music played. The blinking lights would drive me nuts. Some callers wanted to request a song. I would lie and say I'd try to play it. And if their request *did* play during my shift, and I mentioned their names on-air, I became their new best friend and they called every week. Some callers had been on hold waiting for the psychiatrists to give them some advice. When the frazzled callers stopped talking long enough for me to tell them I wasn't the doctor, they'd either make a song request or ask *me* for my advice. I just gave them my honest opinion. It was the early version of "Ask Anita", my popular advice show to come.

The first time I slipped on the headphones and turned on the microphone I knew I had found my place in the world. It was on the radio. I started to get noticed in Philadelphia, and I was

interviewed for the local newspapers. The ratings

were very good. I had regular listeners who called

me every day. For the first time in my life I realized

I was funny. I started to receive fan mail, mostly

from men, including the inmates at Graterford

 Prison, located

about thirty

miles west of

Philadelphia. I

had mixed

feelings about

my new title: "Miss So Fine". Apparently all of

cellblock 400 voted for me.   My dad had to see it to

believe it.

My beginner's luck extended to my first mentors: general manager Jim Keating, program director R.J. Laurence, and music director C.J. Morgan. They decided to make me the "morning

man" when I had no experience. They understood my sense of humor and saw something in me that I never did. Jim, R.J., and C.J. believed in me even when I said stupid things on and off the air.

The end of the seventies was a long time ago and women with careers were big news. On November 14, 1977 an interview I gave to Leslie Bennetts appeared in the Focus section of the *Philadelphia Bulletin*. (Leslie went on to bigger things. In 1988 she became a contributing editor at

Vanity Fair magazine.) Leslie made me feel at ease and before I realized it, I said things I wish I hadn't. Leslie didn't misquote me, but she had a way of "bimbo-izing" me. Here are a few highlights of the three-page article titled WHO'S TUNED IN AND TURNED ON? ANITA. Leslie gives me props and calls me an overnight success. She calls me the broadcast school dropout in the enviable position of frontrunner in the morning radio ratings race. Leslie points out that I'm the first woman to host a local music radio show in the morning and that the ratings have doubled in a matter of months. I am the top rated on-air personality among all adults in the eighteen-to-thirty-four year-old range during my 6 to 10 A.M. shift. Leslie goes on to say: "Anita Gevinson on the air is pretty much the same as Anita Gevinson off the air, uninhibited, funny and a wee bit screwball." My boss Jim Keating is quoted as saying that I have "a naïve sensuality and a bubbly, unpredictable spontaneity."

Then I started talking. I'm quoted as saying "I don't think I had a thought in my head until after I was twenty-one." When asked about living in Mexico, Leslie quotes me saying, "It was real different from living in Levittown." When I told Leslie about my stint as a photographer in Las Vegas, she described me as sashaying around "in my push-up bra and ruffled panties." The article goes on and on to say, aside from national stardom, I want to marry and have children:

> My schedule doesn't leave
>
> much time for romance,
>
> but that's okay, since Anita
>
> doesn't have anyone to go
>
> out with anyway. She
>
> hasn't had to fend off

suitors in the past either. "I never had to turn down a marriage proposal," Anita sighs. "Nobody ever asked me. Sometimes I pick up the phone to see if it's still working." However, if Anita Gevinson's current social calendar leaves something to be desired, at least life in general is more interesting than during the pre-radio career days, when she was once so bored, she had her feet operated on for diversion.

I cried after I read it and swore I would do better next time.

On December 5, 1977 I was featured in the *Philadelphia Journal*, along with Ramona Brabham and Diane Blackmon in a piece by Debra S. Davis. The headline read WCAU'S ANGELS, THREE WOMEN STEPPIN' TO FASCINATING RHYTHM.

WCAU'S ANGELS
Three Women Steppin to Fascinating Rhythm

Ramona, an exotic black woman, is described as having marble like eyes and a soft, mellow, almost hypnotizing voice. She refuses to talk about her social life and only admits to having a man and being divorced. Ramona doesn't sell sex on the air, only words and feelings. She's called sensible and careful not to offend.

Diane is described as a cross between Diana Ross and Lola Falana with an ego that just won't quit. Her show is called the "Diane Blackmon Experience". She was the first woman on the air at WCAU-FM and is characterized as distinctively funky. She's an up person and her goal is to have a Dinah Shore type show. Diane, who's 25 and has an eight-year-old son says, "Listen, you have to be better than men. It will just be a little while until women take over or at least get into management positions."

My interview starts with the headline THE MORNING MAN AT WCAU-FM IS A WOMAN. I'm described as having a kicky delivery and a friendly voice. I'm called "something different", "unpredictable," and "off the wall". My show is called the hottest morning show for young adults in the Delaware Valley. I'm "knocking holes in the morning man tradition." It all sounded so good. Why oh why did I have to open my mouth? After spending some time with me, the interviewer reveals these gems: "Anita hates getting up in the morning and it's her worst time of the day." "Even though she spins the discs for a club hopping audience,

Anita has an idle social life." "Anita has to be in bed by 10

P.M. to make that 4:30 alarm." Then I'm quoted as saying,

"I've had bad relationships with men. They want to be the

boss. I've got enough bosses here at the studio."

I was so embarrassed by the interview but no one

else thought it was bad at all. In fact my bosses loved

seeing their names in the paper and my parents were

beyond proud. And so I was happy at last and I had a job I

would have done for free. I thought the money I was

making was way too much, but I had no trouble spending

every cent, and then some. I moved out of a terrible

apartment with no security on 12th & Locust Street (or 12th

& Lust as I called it), into a high rise with too much

security called "Park Town Place". It's one of the

apartment buildings in the background of the *Rocky* movie

when he runs up the steps at the Philadelphia Museum of

Art. I learned that as a DJ I didn't have to pay for dinner or

concert tickets and I had a backstage pass to every concert.

I got all the albums for free weeks before anyone else. In 1977 disco music ruled the airwaves. The movie *Saturday Night Fever* was a giant at the box office and the soundtrack sounded great along with The Commodores, Thelma Houston, Stevie Wonder, and The Emotions.

I knew the odds of someone like me getting their first radio job in a city like Philadelphia were slim to none. The fact that this was happening to me seemed impossible only a few years ago. Getting paid to spend four or five hours a day listening to music is a very fun way to live. I was so happy in the studio that I sang along to each song I played. My singing voice is close to but definitely not on key. But that has never stopped me from belting out every song like Liza Minnelli.

2

Music was a big part of my life from the time I was a kid growing up in the Philadelphia suburb of Levittown, Pennsylvania. If you lived in the tri-state area (Pennsylvania, New Jersey, and Delaware) in the sixties, you grew up listening to rock 'n' roll and R&B music equally. Instead of enjoying the beach in Atlantic City, New Jersey, I spent many sizzling, humid hours standing in line waiting to get into the ballroom at The Steel Pier. I saw The Animals, featuring a very angry looking Eric Burdon wearing the first dungaree jacket I ever saw. The stage was filled with trashcans and they sat on top of them while singing "We Gotta Get Out of This Place". Eric Burdon was the first rock star to scare me a little bit, and I liked the way that felt. When I saw the Temptations, David Ruffin whipped me into such a frenzy that I rushed the stage in the middle of "My Girl". I took off my pink plastic bubble ring and threw it at him. When I saw Gerry and the Pacemakers and they sang "Ferry Cross the Mercey", I was sobbing. I thought Peter Noone of Herman's Hermits was so cute that after their show I followed the crowd of girls to their hotel. I ran through the lobby and got into the elevator. When the security guards chased me away I slipped into the stairwell. After a couple of hours I realized that Herman and his Hermits were not going to let me into their room.

This would not be the night of my first sexual experience.

In retrospect, the shows I saw on the Steel Pier were much more memorable than losing my virginity. (It was a lifeguard by the way, under the boardwalk in Atlantic City, but nothing like the song by the Drifters.)

I never missed a performance of a rock 'n' roll band on *The Ed Sullivan Show*. The Beatles, The Rolling Stones, and even The Doors were in my living room and it was very exciting. My favorite movie was *Bye Bye Birdie* wherein the hot rock god Conrad Birdie comes to a small town and changes the life of a girl played by Ann-Margaret. The movie ends with Conrad performing on *The Ed Sullivan Show*. I would think about it every time I was just offstage watching a concert by the rock star of the month. Everyone in the audience wanted to be with him, but I was the one he left with in the limo.

I used my allowance to buy all the records that I heard on the radio. I skipped Hebrew school and stayed home to watch *The Monkees* on television. The Monkees' concert in Philadelphia was my first. I took a shoebox full of chocolate chip cookies that my mom made. They were for Davy Jones, my favorite Monkee, and I wore my favorite "bloomer dress" in the "Mod, Mod World" style of the day. Instead of playing with others during recess, I stood in the playground's shade holding a transistor radio to my ear, hoping to hear "I Want to Hold Your Hand" for the tenth time that day. I started a Beatles fan club with just two members—a girl who loved Paul and me, the John lover—because I didn't want any competition.

Philadelphia is known as a great radio city. I think of it as The City of Brotherly Love of All Music. No matter which part of the city or suburbs you came from, there was a natural appreciation of musical styles, from the Temptations to Hall & Oates, the Delphonics to the O'Jays, Billy Joel to Bruce Springsteen. The Rolling Stones and David Bowie would start their stadium tours in Philadelphia. I think it's because the Philly audiences always "had their backs" through the dreaded new songs and sound glitches. We show up for the opening act and hardly ever boo them off the stage. We stay until the end of the show and demand an encore, even if the house lights are turned on and we have to work the next day. We're always up for a sing-a-long; we all know all the words.

And in my youth we could dance, since we all grew up watching *American Bandstand*, Philly's very own after school dance party. Every day after school I watched, while my mother ironed. I dreamed of the day I turned thirteen, and was old enough to dance on the show. Unlike my excited parents, I wasn't looking forward to my Bat Mitzvah. In fact I hoped to borrow a Catholic school uniform from my friend because all the best dancers on *American Bandstand* wore Catholic school uniforms.

My early fascination with all things Catholic stemmed from watching Haley Mills in the movie *The Trouble with Angels*. I wanted to be that girl in that boarding school mixing it up with all those nuns. Just like Haley Mills, I got into trouble when I went to Sunday morning mass with my friend's large Catholic family. Her parents didn't notice me slip into their station wagon. I walked into the church with a big smile on my face, crossed myself backwards, and said a very loud "Amen." My friend's parents looked over at me and smiled. They all stood up and I thought it was time to leave. I followed them toward the front of the church and to my surprise they fell on their knees. I tried to look like I'd done this before. The priest started walking toward me carrying some sort of smoking incense. Everyone on their knees around me stuck out their tongues, so I did the same. The priest dropped something into the open mouths and I started to panic. I thought I had to say something. When the priest was about to drop something on my outstretched tongue I blurted out "I'm Jewith." The priest just stared at me. "I'm Jewith," I tried to say again. The priest frowned. I closed my eyes and in a second tasted something sweet. To my amazement, lightning didn't strike me. I went home and told my parents I'd been baptized. My mother told me to go to my room and study my haftorah.

In 1964, I was twelve years old when Dick Clark's *American Bandstand* relocated to Los Angeles. I was crushed when I realized I would never dance on the show surrounded by girls in Catholic school outfits. Eventually I forgave Dick Clark and continued to watch *American Bandstand* on television, along with my other favorites, *Shindig!*, *Hullabaloo*, and *Soul Train*. I still remember the night I saw the Kinks perform that guitar solo during "You Really Got Me". I wanted to be one of the dancers in the background with the go-go boots and long straight hair.

When I got to high school, I still had a need to dance in public, even though my moves were awful. (Think Elaine from *Seinfeld*.) On weekends, I went to one of two dances hosted by local radio personalities Jerry Blavat, who called himself "the Geator with the Heator" or "the Boss with the Hot Sauce", and Ron Cutler, better known as Ron Diamond, the "Atomic Mouth". Before radio, Jerry Blavat did everything from managing bands like Danny and the Juniors, who had a hit with "At the Hop", to working as Don Rickles's valet. Blavat got his start in radio in 1960 and by 1963 he had a syndicated show and hosted dances at schools like St. Francis of Assisi in Ventnor, New Jersey. I practiced my moves to his weekly show called "The Discophonic Scene". In 1962 Ron Diamond was hosting dances at the Starlight Ballroom and by 1966 he had the number one radio show on WTTM. His dances were attended by hundreds of kids. These DJs were bigger local stars than the television newscasters.

When I went to the Ron Diamond dance at the Edgely Fire Hall near Bristol, Pennsylvania, I made my mom drop me off a block away. I told her it was because I was embarrassed that my mom had to drive me to the dance, but it was really because I didn't want her to see the boys being frisked at the door for weapons. My new black leather jacket was stolen the first time I wore it. My mom wouldn't let me go there again. It was just as well. I was sixteen years old and started to dress like Janis Joplin.

My first life-changing concert was Janis Joplin with Big Brother and the Holding Company at The Electric Factory at 22nd and Arch Streets in Philadelphia. The Electric Factory venue was a converted warehouse that opened in 1968. The five men who built it—Jerry, Allen and Herb Spivak, Shelley Kaplan, and Larry Magid—set the stage (pun intended) for Philadelphia to become a powerful concert town.

Before the Electric Factory, musicians gathered in Rittenhouse Square and on Samson Street in coffeehouses like Gilded Cage and The Second Fret. There was a "psychedelic" club called Kaleidoscope, which was an old movie theatre on Main Street in Manayunk, right outside of Philadelphia. Manny Rubin, the owner of The Second Fret, later opened a club on Sansom Street called The Trauma. Local bands Mandrake Memorial and Woody's Truck Stop, featuring a guy from Upper Darby, Pennsylvania named Todd Rundgren, played there. In 1966 Joni Mitchell performed at the Second Fret when she was still married to Chuck Mitchell.

By 1968 all the rock 'n' roll bands were coming to Philadelphia to play. When the Electric Factory opened in February 1968, the Chambers Brothers were the headliners. The Jimi Hendrix Experience performed two shows each night at the Electric Factory on February 21 and 22. The opening act was Woody's Truck Stop. Country Joe and the Fish played on March 1, 2, and 3, and Janis Joplin with Big Brother and the Holding Company came to town for two shows on March 15 and 17.

I took the train from Levittown to 30th Street Station in Philadelphia and walked to the Electric Factory. When I entered the dark smoky theatre I was temporarily blinded by throbbing strobe lights and spinning mirror balls. I staggered through a foggy tunnel filled with black lights, Day-Glo paint, and a guy in a gorilla suit. I found a seat on the floor just as Janis took the stage. The band started playing "Piece of my Heart", Janis took a swig of Wild Turkey, and at that moment I swore I'd find a way to see every rock 'n' roll band that came to town.

In May I went to see Iron Butterfly at the Electric Factory. I had to be home by midnight, which meant I had to take the 11 P.M. train and I'd *still* be a half hour late. At ten-thirty Iron Butterfly was in the middle of the "In-A-Gadda-Da-Vida" drum solo. I knew it could be at least fifteen minutes before the song ended. Reluctantly I had to leave. I stood up and tripped over several people seated on the floor. The spotlight was shining on me and I could hear people grumbling all the way to the door. I was humiliated but I made my train.

In July 1969 I went to my first "Be-In" with Boyfriend #1. The "Be-In", also the brainchild of the Electric Factory guys, was a free Sunday afternoon concert at Belmont Plateau in Philly's Fairmount Park. It started at noon and the stage was set up in the back of a pickup truck.

The food was free. I wore my favorite outfit: a shiny leopard skin halter top, bell bottoms, and red clogs. Boyfriend #1 and I made out on a blanket all day and smoked a lot of pot.

The Atlantic City Pop Festival, also the brainchild of Larry Magid and The Spivaks, was scheduled for August 1, 2 and 3 that same year, twelve days after Neil Armstrong and Buzz Aldrin walked on the moon and two weeks before Woodstock. My mother refused to let me go to Woodstock. She told me to forget about it since she was sure that "no one would schlep all the way to upstate New York to go to a rock 'n' roll show." Since my mother spent many formative years in Atlantic City, she encouraged me to go to the Atlantic City Pop Festival instead. Tickets cost $6.75 for one day or fifteen dollars for all three days. My dad agreed to drive me to the racetrack and I could stay for *one day* until 11 P.M., no sleeping over.

On August 2 my dad dropped me off at the festival and I ran from the car as he yelled more instructions. The line-up for the day's concert was Creedence Clearwater Revival, Lighthouse, B.B. King, Butterfield Blues Band, Tim Buckley, The Byrds, Hugh Masekela, American Dream, the Crazy World of Arthur Brown, and Jefferson Airplane. Once again I had to leave early so I could meet my dad at 11 P.M. As I started walking up the steps to leave I heard the crowd go crazy. I turned around and saw Grace Slick had taken off her shirt. Years later I would get to tell Jefferson Airplane's Marty Balin that story and also ask Carl Palmer if he played drums for Arthur Brown that day. Years later, when I was naked and in bed with each of them, I asked them all about it.

Philadelphia's WMMR was one of the original rock stations in the country. It was the first of the east coast stations to play music from the Grateful Dead, Van Halen, and U2. I'd been tuned in since 1970. I would sit in the parking lot of Bucks County Community College in Newtown, Pennsylvania (or "Buck U" as we called it) in my red P1800S Volvo smoking hash and listening to WMMR. I never missed Dave Herman's show called "The Marconi Experiment". The theme song was "Flying" by the Beatles and over the intro Dave would recite the words of Khalil Gibran: "Arise my heart and fill your voice with music. For he who shares not dawn with his song, is one of the sons of ever darkness." Carol Miller was the only girl disc jockey I heard on the radio. She was on WMMR in 1972 while she attended the University of Pennsylvania. A year later, Carol was attending law school and working at WNEW in New York.

On WMMR you could hear everything from Quicksilver Messenger Service to Country Joe Macdonald and the Fish to Ken Nordine. The Philly airwaves also had WDAS-FM 105.3, Philly's Best R&B and Classic Soul station. In 1959 WDAS played rock music and, on Sundays only, classical music. Then it was 100 percent classical until 1968 when it changed back to Rock. It was the age of "underground" or "progressive" FM radio and the disc jockeys included Hy Lit, Jay Mark (who went on to Sigma Sound Studios and became an award-winning sound mixer), and future WMMR jocks Gene Shay, Michael Tearson, Steve Martorano, and Ed Sciaky.

In the late sixties through the early seventies the Nixon administration was censoring music on the radio that involved drug content. The FCC tried to get WDAS station owner Max Leon's son Steve, who called himself "my father's son", to remove the offending tunes. Instead, he played Arlo Guthrie's "Coming into Los Angeles". Max Leon flew into a rage, trashed the studio, then fired his son and the entire air staff. In 1971 WDAS played only R&B music and launched the careers of The O'Jays, Teddy Pendergrass, and Lou Rawls. The DJs were stars in their own right. For example, Georgie Woods, "the Guy with the

Goods". Georgie broke (meaning played for the first time) Sam Cooke's "You Send Me" in 1957. He nicknamed Jerry Butler "The Iceman" because he was so cool onstage. In 1962 Georgie played the Beatles' "Please Please Me" solely because it was on the Vee Jay label, the same record company that Jerry Butler recorded for. In 1964 Georgie coined the phrase "blue-eyed soul" for the Righteous Brothers.

Some of the best radio stories are about Philadelphia DJs like Long John Wade, who was given an early copy of the *White Album* from John Lennon. Since WFIL, where Long John worked at the time, couldn't play the Beatles or any rock music, he gave it to Ed Sciaky to play for his listeners first. Ed was Billy Joel and Bruce Springsteen's earliest and most vocal supporter. In 1972 WMMR aired a live concert featuring Billy Joel from a small club called The Main Point. Dennis Wilen was the music director and to ensure a full house he made sure

WMMR listeners were given tickets to the show. That night Billy Joel performed "Captain Jack" for the first time.

Levittown, Pennsylvania is seventy-two miles away from New York but at night I could pick up the signal from WABC-AM 770, with the insanely popular line-up of Dan Ingram, Charlie Greer, Ron Lundy, and my favorite Bruce Morrow a.k.a. "Cousin Brucie". I was raised on some of the best radio ever and I couldn't have gone through puberty without them.

The life of a radio DJ seemed to be very cool, but I never thought of doing it myself. In those days all the DJs were near-exclusively men. There was no such thing as a girl sidekick. I never sat alone in my basement pretending I was doing a show on the radio. I never practiced my autograph or thought about what my "radio name" would be. In truth, I was hoping to become an airline stewardess. In 1965 I saw a movie called *Boeing Boeing* starring Tony Curtis and Jerry Lewis. They played airline pilots who dated three beautiful stewardesses. I loved the uniforms and I wanted to see the world, so that was my dream job. Instead, I did a lot of waiting tables. I could always get hired to be a waitress, even though I did it very badly. The worst experience I had was at the Blue Fountain Diner on Old Lincoln Highway in Langhorne, Pennsylvania. It lasted less than an hour. The manager let me have the counter customers since that's the easiest job. My first customer ordered some sort of mystery meat and I had to go into the kitchen and pretend I knew what it was. I stood at the counter forever waiting for my order. Finally I had to beg the cooks to help me identify it. It was cold by the time I figured it out. As I begged the cooks to make another one, the manager walked in. There were a bunch of angry customers waiting at the counter so he fired me. I still don't know what braised short ribs look like.

Then there was a disastrous five minutes playing Santa Claus. That's how long it took for the first kid that sat on my lap to scream "She's not Santa, she's *a girl!*" I worked several jobs in clothing stores at shopping malls. I sold blue jeans to men at a store called Willie Lump Lump. If you wanted your jeans tailored or shortened I'd give you a "chalk job", and measure your inseam while I was on my knees wearing hot pants. I was nineteen years old and the minimum wage was about $1.60 an hour. A gallon of gas cost about a quarter, and my cigarette of choice, Marlboros (only in the box), cost thirty-five cents a pack. After barely graduating from Neshaminy Senior High School in Langhorne in 1970, and two years at Bucks County Community College, I didn't have any career goals. Instead, I wanted to take a journey, just like every other happy hippie. I knew there had to be more to life than Levittown.

Levittown, Pennsylvania is located between Philadelphia and Trenton, New Jersey. Downtown Philly, or Center City, is about twenty-two miles away. Levittown was built in 1952 by Levitt and Sons, and they were also

the builders of Levittown, New Jersey (before it became

Willingboro) and Levittown, New York, the childhood

home of Billy Joel. Billy's song "Allentown" was

originally called "Levittown". Levittown's modest houses

were moderately priced and only required a down payment

of a thousand dollars. It's no wonder why my parents

decided to leave my dad's hometown of Washington, D.C.

and move back to my mom's turf when I was two years

old.

Levittown had a lot of unspoken rules when I was

growing up. No black people and few Jewish families

moved into the neighborhood. I was oblivious to the racism

and had a wonderful time on Nasturtium Lane. Once I

memorized how to spell it. My family's two-story house

was filled with loving parents and lots of music, including

Broadway show tunes, Frank Sinatra, Judy Garland, Barbra

Streisand, Steve Lawrence, and Edie Gorme. I could

usually be found in my room playing my Beatles and Rolling Stone albums. My friends always came over to our house after school to dance in the living room. I would bring my Temptations and Four Tops records downstairs and put them on the big stereo.

My dad worked two jobs so we could have everything we needed. He was a grocery buyer for the Food Fair supermarket chain in an office building in downtown Philadelphia, right across the street from Amtrak's 30th Street Station. On the weekends he sold men's clothing at Robert Hall's. Money was still tight, and our family vacations were generally spent camping in the Jersey Pines, but when I was about twelve years old we went to New York to see all the best Broadway shows. My parents and my younger sister were equally excited when we went to the 1964-1965 World's Fair in Queens, New York. I was particularly thrilled to find out that my dad had some sort of connection and his name was on a special list so we didn't have to wait in line. The perk was the best part of the visit. Not the Unisphere, the twelve-story high, stainless steel model of the Earth. Not the Vatican Pavilion, where Michelangelo's "Pietà" was displayed, or Dinoland, featuring life-size replicas of nine different dinosaurs. For me, it was cutting the line. I decided I would have a job someday that allowed me special treatment.

My mom and dad had a wonderful marriage but limited parenting skills. "We only had Dr. Spock," my mother would say in her defense. Mom's words of wisdom when it came to love were "Men are like trolley cars—if you miss the first one, another will show up in fifteen minutes." My dad never commented on things like sex or love, and he let my mother do most of the talking. They were obviously very much in love and they never fought and hardly ever argued. As for our Jewish heritage, my Mother had a "one size fits all" explanation of all the Jewish customs and holidays. Whenever I asked her why we did the things we did at Passover, Rosh Hashanah,

Chanukah, or Yom Kipper, she would say the same thing:

"They tried to kill us; we survived. Let's eat."

(Later when I got my first radio job my mother gave

me this advice about show business: "Never follow a banjo

act because they bring the

house down.")

My parents were

supportive of anything I

wanted to do as long as it made

me happy, didn't cost too

much, and didn't hurt anyone.

That included my ever-changing choice of hairstyles,

clothes, and boyfriends. I met my first full-time boyfriend

while I was working in a fast food biker hangout called

Steer Inn. Boyfriend #1 was blond and had a body like

Michelangelo's "David". He was able to look past the

awful uniform I had to wear (a cowboy hat and checkered shirt) and I was able to look past his heroin habit.

There were some good things about Boyfriend #1. I was seventeen and living at home and he was twenty-three and had an apartment on 4th and Pine streets in Philadelphia. He took me to South Street where I discovered an exotic new world. I met two handsome, elegant, gay men, Garrick Melmeck and his lover Xavier Hussenet, aka "ZaZa". In 1970 they opened a nightclub called La Banane Noire (Black Banana) on 534 South 4th street. It moved to 3rd and Race streets and became a private club called The Crusaders Community Club. Cafe ZaZa served food while the Black Banana was a decadent after hours club. Garrick and Xavier lived in a three-story brownstone on South Street. The first floor was an artsy boutique called Gazoo, where they sold art by locals. The hash we smoked there was definitely not local.

Boyfriend #1 was a part-time student at the Philadelphia College of Art and he suggested I pose as a nude model for an art class. It was scary but I walked into the class wearing only a bathrobe and climbed onto the small platform in the center of the room. The students sat in a circle around me. I sat down on a folding chair and slipped off the robe. Everyone started sketching and no one made eye contact. After a few nauseous minutes I was able to relax. I felt more like Anita Pallenberg than Anita Gevinson.

Boyfriend #1 took me to the Philadelphia Folk Festival in Schwenksville, PA, where I finally got to have my fuck in the mud "Woodstock" experience. On our way to see the movie *Easy Rider* we had to stop at the Methadone clinic. I waited in the car wondering what the hell was going on. I had never met anyone who did heroin and had never heard of Methadone. Boyfriend #1 didn't fit the junkie profile. He looked healthy and didn't do any other drugs or drink liquor. Except for falling asleep as if he had narcolepsy and those burn marks on the bottom of the teaspoons in my mother's kitchen, you would never know.

I had to lie to my parents about a lot of things and I wasn't very good at it. One evening I was upstairs getting ready for Boyfriend #1 to pick me up when I heard my parents talking.

"Phil, he's taking her out tonight," my mother informed my dad.

"Who's paying?" my ever trusting dad asked as I started down the stairs.

"It's good that you're getting away from that hangout," said my ever optimistic mother.

"But Ma, I *work* there," I whined.

"You call that work, wearing a cowboy hat, serving hamburgers to hippies?" my dad asked, shaking his head.

"Oh Phil, she looks cute in that hat," my mother said and beamed.

Dad looked at me in my leopard skin halter top and no bra and shook his head again.

"You think this boyfriend is the right one for you?" he asked.

"How would I know?" I shrieked. "I'm seventeen and know nothing and you're Einstein."

"Don't get fresh," my mother warned.

"Gotta go, he's here." I started toward the door.

"Isn't he going to come in?"

"No. And Ma, get away from the window. He'll see you in your muumuu."

As I ran down the driveway I heard my mother say, "Look he's driving a foreign car."

My mother is truly the most optimistic person in the world. She refuses to see the bad in anyone and refuses to believe anyone is capable of doing terrible things. She hates it when I tell people she wants to hear Hitler's side before she judges him. At first, I didn't tell my parents that I had started seeing Boyfriend #1. One night I told my parents I was going to meet some girls at the mall and see a movie. Instead I went to Boyfriend #1's apartment and we made love for hours. When I came home my mother was sitting in the den watching TV. I sat down and we had a short conversation about the movie I didn't see. A couple more lies later I faked a yawn and said goodnight. Once I was in my room I looked in the mirror and saw that my sweater was inside out. I didn't know whether to laugh or cry. My mother never said a word about it. She let my guilt punish me.

Despite his heroin intake, Boyfriend #1 could screw all night, but I knew I couldn't stay with him. He confused jealousy with love and was possessive and needy. I hate needy. One day I walked down the hall of Neshaminy High School and saw him in a fist fight with the Dean of Students. I felt embarrassed and was extremely relieved when I barely graduated in 1970. Instead of getting a new boyfriend I thought it would be better if I got my own place. I moved into a house with two girls I'd met after enrolling in Bucks County Community College. The house in Langhorne only had two bedrooms so we flipped a coin and, luckily, I wasn't the one that had to move her mattress into the closet. Boyfriend #1 got a job as a mover and most mornings my roommates and I would find random furniture on the front yard. I drew the line at receiving stolen goods. I knew I had to break it off. We were sitting in his father's Saab when I told him it was over and he told me no one would ever love me the way he did.

I prayed that he was right.

I met Boyfriend #2 at Bucks County Community college. He was in the cafeteria eating a "Bucks Burger" and he was blond and looked a lot like Boyfriend #1. It made for an easy transition.

Boyfriend #2 told me he was getting a divorce after a brief marriage. Right out of the Navy, he was uptight and sexually  deprived and deeply in need of a makeover. I showed him the man he could be and after a couple of months he seemed to really like himself. After we graduated from the two-year college we decided to transfer to a college in Mexico. Boyfriend #2 had spent his honeymoon in Mexico and wanted to go back. I had never been there but it sounded good to me. When we told my parents our plan, my father asked "What's wrong with Temple University?"

At times both of my parents could sound like " borscht belt" stand-up comics.

"There won't be any temples where they're going," my mother said in her best Shecky Green impersonation.

On December 20, 1972, Boyfriend #2 and I left Levittown in his yellow Fiat Spider convertible. We each brought one suitcase and a shitload of black hash. He drove and I kept the pipe full and we smoked our way across the country. When we crossed the border into Mexico at Nuevo Laredo, Texas, the border patrol took most of the cash we had on us. I was sure this was more of an "America" thing than a "Mexico" thing and I was happy to be in a better place..

3

Universidad de las Americas is located in the town of
Cholula, eighty miles south of Mexico City near the big
city of Puebla. It's about 7,050 feet above sea level (as if I
wasn't high enough). According to the *Guinness Book of
World Records*, the great pyramid of Cholula is the largest
pyramid, as well as the largest monument ever constructed
anywhere in the world. It has a base of 1476 x 1476 feet
and a height of 217 feet. The Aztec Indians believed that
Xelhus, a giant, built the pyramid. Today there is a church
called Iglesia de Nuestra Senora de los Remedies (Church
of Our Lady of the Remedies). It's a major Catholic
pilgrimage destination so I was especially excited about
going there since I still held onto my fascination with all
things Catholic.

Como se dice "culture shock" *en Espanol?*

Cholula's beauty was as shocking as its poverty.
The sunsets were spectacular. The people were friendly and
warm. And the weather was perfect. The Aztec Indians
were especially kind and they speak their own language
called Nahuatl. The women do all the work and are strong
enough to carry buckets of water in each hand and, oh
yeah, they're barefoot. The volcano, Mt. Popo, short for
Popocatepetl, means "smoking mountain" in Nahuatl. I
loved the smell of the buses exhaust fumes mixed with the

freshly made tortillas. I loved the street food even though I often didn't know what the hell I was eating and knew I'd likely be sick in a couple of hours. The fruit was so good it was like tasting cantaloupe and pineapple for the first time. The *liquados* I had every morning were like a fruit explosion in my mouth. The pot was *spectacular* and so cheap it was insane. (Wait, maybe *that's* why everything tasted so good.) *Sensimilla* became one of my first Spanish words. A big ice chest full of it cost fifteen dollars, and you could buy Quaaludes in every farmacia.

Boyfriend #2 and I found an apartment in Cholula near the college. The rent was fifty dollars a month. There was no refrigerator and no heat so we bought a clay oven and burned wood. If it rained, which it hardly ever did, we had running water. And we had electricity for most of the day, but hardly ever at night. There was one pizza parlor/disco in town called Pollo's and a million little bars. We found a better apartment and Boyfriend #2 built a bed for us to sleep in. I wanted to love living with him, but I didn't. I had never lived with anyone as "a couple" and I didn't like the pressure. Some days I simply wanted to be alone.

We enrolled in the Universidad de las Americas. My major was self-medication. Sometimes I'd show up for a photography or Spanish class but most of my time was spent going to different farmacias to buy Quaaludes. Boyfriend #2 and I started to hang out with a girl from New York and her Texan boyfriend. On Fridays we would all drive to exotic beaches in magical places like Veracruz, Oaxaca, or Puerto Escondido. Back in Cholula, we'd wait and watch the weather. If it rained on a Tuesday or Wednesday, Psilocybin mushrooms would be ready to sell by Friday. The dealers came from another small town called Cuautla, which was a couple of hours away. They would hide the "magic" mushrooms wrapped in T-shirts rolled up in their sombreros. When they got off the bus they came directly to our apartment. All the students would stop by to buy the "shrooms" and head for the pyramid.

I just couldn't swallow the shit (literally) that the mushrooms are grown in no matter how many times I tried. Instead I'd pop a Quaalude and play my David Bowie and Bob Dylan tapes for the travelling mushroom dealers. We'd howl with laughter as they tried to sing along to Bowie's "Changes". I couldn't eat the mushrooms but I did love drinking the powerful, homemade Aguardiente. I also loved the region's churches, bars, beer, and even language, though I was having trouble learning it.

After a few months, I started to notice that Boyfriend #2 was attracted to more than a couple of the girls we met. And I was pretty sure he was sleeping with the girl from New York. To be fair, I was also looking around, and had a tryst with my photography teacher in the darkroom. I also spent an afternoon in the bed of Leopolo de la Rosa, the owner of the disco Pollo's. The sex was great and I didn't feel guilty. I knew my relationship with Boyfriend #2 was all but over. Still, my ego got in the way and I lost it when Boyfriend #2 told me he had fallen in love with a girl he'd just met. I was so hurt I had to get out of there.

I said goodbye to Mexico and went back to Levittown.

The reentry was brutal. I was angry and missed Mexico but surprisingly not Boyfriend #2 as much. Determined never to be a waitress again, I got a job at a local mall selling unisex clothing. The boutique was called "No Name" and I was hired to be the assistant manager. The store's walls were painted black and the clothes were ridiculous. I blasted David Bowie's *Ziggy Stardust and the Spiders from Mars* album and stood behind the cash register with a scowl on my face. I hated my job and the mall's overbearing air conditioning. And did I mention that

I was back living at home with my parents? I didn't think anything could bring me out of my funk.

Then I discovered Bruce Springsteen and the E Street Band.

I was working in the unisex boutique one day when I saw a guy schlepping a snack tray and a box of tickets. He wanted to sell them in the front of the store. I asked him whom the concert was for and he said, "Bruce Springsteen." I thought I knew who Bruce was but I was confusing him with Norman Greenbaum. Springsteen, Greenbaum. "Spirit in the Night", "Spirit in the Sky". You can see how easily that could happen. Plus I'd been in Mexico, so I missed Springsteen's February shows at the Main Point in Bryn Mawr, including the one that aired on WMMR.

For some reason I let the guy set up his little table in the front of the store and sell the tickets. When the manager found out, I was fired. Feeling responsible, the ticket guy

offered me a job selling tickets for this band from Jersey.

With no other immediate options, I accepted. I filled my car

with posters, a roll of masking tape, and a box of tickets

and off I drove to New Hope, Pennsylvania, one of those

little artsy touristy towns. There I went into the nightclub

John & Peter's and took a seat at the bar. I had once been a

waitress there too and thus knew they hosted live bands. I

figured I could convince the bartender to sell the tickets. He

said he'd do it as a favor to me.

The tickets cost two dollars and he didn't sell many.

I saw Bruce Springsteen and the E Street Band

perform for the first time at the State Theatre in New

Brunswick, New Jersey on April 19, 1974. The place seated

five hundred but only about half of the tickets were sold. I

got there early and stood in the box office hoping to sell

some more tickets. The band started rehearsing and I was

drawn to the stage. They were playing "Twist and Shout"

and it sounded spectacular. I couldn't take my eyes off the frail, raspy voiced singer.

This was definitely not Norman Greenbaum.

Bruce started his now famous count of "One, two, three, four" and took the band through "Quarter to Three". The band seemed satisfied and started to pack up but Bruce wanted to do it again. He seemed to care a little too much. This was, after all, only sound check. But Bruce knew what he was doing and the shows I was about to witness made me a concert fanatic.

That night I was standing in the aisle watching the sound check when Clarence Clemons walked to the edge of the stage and motioned to me to come closer. He kneeled down and said, "When my wife gets here, make sure you let her in right away and take her backstage, okay?"

"Yes, of course," I stammered.

Clarence looked around cautiously and then moved even closer to me and said, "And when my *girlfriend* gets here, make sure she gets in right away but don't let her go backstage." He flashed that big smile and I promised him I'd do it.

David Sancious was in the E Street Band then. He played the keyboard parts on the *Greetings from Asbury Park* album. And that's David on the brilliant organ solo on "Kitty's Back" and the intro for "New York City Serenade". David was born in Asbury Park, New Jersey and the band practiced in his family's house when he lived in Belmont on E Street. When drummer Vini "Mad Dog" Lopez left the band, David's friend Ernie "Boom Boom" Carter took his place. That night, the set list was long and the band seemed to get tired of playing long before Bruce. The audience grew restless when Bruce stopped in the middle of a song to tell a story. He was heckled by someone in the sparse audience who yelled "Shut up and sing!" Bruce lost his cool and yelled "Fuck you" at the heckler, who then threw his folding chair at the stage. I didn't care about any of that. I was mesmerized and thought Bruce and the band were incredible. I vowed to spread the word.

On May 6 I saw my second Springsteen show at my alma mater, Bucks County Community College. I decided to break out my camera for the first time since I'd left Mexico. I stood on the side of the stage and got some great shots of Bruce. I did it again at the May 24th show at the Trenton War Memorial. Return to Forever with Chick Corea opened the show. It was Bob Dylan's birthday and Bruce sort of morphed into Bob that night. I knew I wasn't the Boss's type but it was impossible to not have sex dreams about him anyway. Sometimes when he was onstage I would imagine how long he could fuck since Bruce seemed to have endless energy. Even his band had had enough after about three hours, so Bruce often performed the encore alone. One night he played "For You" and accompanied himself on the piano. I was so moved I forgot I had a camera and stopped shooting.

Here's the set list:

"New York City Serenade"

"Spirit in the Night"

"It's Hard to Be a Saint in the City'

"The E Street Shuffle / Havin' a Party"

"Growin' Up"

"4th of July, Asbury Park (Sandy)"

"Kitty's Back"

"For You"

"Rosalita" (including "Shotgun")

And then it's encore time—a rockin' "Twist and Shout" and "Quarter to Three", followed by "A Love So Fine" and "Wear My Ring Around Your Neck".

It didn't seem like it at the time, but Bruce and the band were going to be just fine. I, on the other hand, was still miserable. As much as I loved going to Bruce shows, I loved Mexico even more. And so on May 29, 1974, I left Levittown again for Cholula.

(Five months later, Bruce Springsteen was famously on the covers of both *Time* and *Newsweek* magazine.)

Back in Mexico, I realized that getting to be there on my own was a better gift than getting the guy. I felt completely free and in 1974 it was possible for a young girl to travel alone and braless without getting murdered. Living in Cholula was a little awkward since everywhere I went I saw my Boyfriend #2 and all of my old friends. I had every intention of going back to school but instead I took a detour. I was looking for a place to live, and I found much more when I knocked on the door of a big two-story house. Two very attractive men lived there, and I couldn't make a choice. Rolando looked like Mick Jagger, and Luis resembled Paul Simon in the early eighties when he was very cute. I was very attracted to both of them and they were fine with that.

Rolando spent most of his time sculpting wood and Luis was a writer who read his poetry aloud every morning at the breakfast table. Luis was moody but a sweet lover and a very nice guy. He and I would have passionate sex in the afternoons and then we'd sit in the big living room and read for hours. It was very soothing and spiritual. I also loved going to the local strip club with Rolando and his crazy pals. I was the only girl patron, and the only American. We always got the table right in front of the stage. A tired waitress would bring over a bottle of

Presidente brandy and four dirty glasses. A really bad three-piece band played something unrecognizable and a naked girl with a large scar on her stomach took the stage and started to go-go dance. Everyone would hoot and holler and throw coins on the stage. It wasn't pretty to watch her bend over to pick them up, but it became really funny after a Quaalude.

After we got home, Rolando and I would have rough sex and as soon as it was over he'd leave and go out again. Rolando was the kind of man who never stayed home and Luis never went out. Remarkably Rolando and Luis didn't mind sharing me and, I have to admit, I loved the attention as much as the sex.

Together, Rolando and Luis made one perfect man.

Of course these hedonistic situations never last. It was too hot not to self-combust and a couple of months later it did, due to egos and surfaced jealousy. As sad as it was to leave those two behind, I knew I had to move on.

I went back to school to sign up for the next semester, but again, I got distracted. His name was Billy, and I met him in the registration line. He was from London, England, and he lived in a big house in Mexico City with his rich parents. His father had a store in the most expensive shopping area, "La Zona Rosa". Billy was crazy about me and I liked the way that felt. I enjoyed watching him try to make his rich parents like me. They never did, but they had a television, a maid, and a cook, and I wanted to move into their house. They made me stay in my own room, but after everyone went to bed I would sneak into Billy's room each night and hope they would walk in on us having sex. I really pissed them off one night at the dinner table. I ate my first artichoke and they almost passed out when I swallowed the whole leaf. I felt I had more in common with their maid and cook and I would spend most of my time sitting in the kitchen talking to them. All in all, not a lot of fun. Once again I knew it was time to move on.

I decided to return to Acapulco, where I had once spent my twenty-first birthday with Boyfriend #2. I loved everything about it, including the name, which means "at the big reeds" in Nahuatl. I tried to explain myself to Billy, who didn't understand why I was leaving. I packed only one suitcase and got on a bus, leaving most of my stuff at Billy's parent's house. Since I had no money and knew no one in Acapulco I thought I would return in a couple of days.

That never happened.

The day I arrived in Acapulco I met a man named Jorge while crossing the street. He looked over at me and grabbed my hand and that was that. Acapulco was a sexy hot spot in the seventies and I loved it there right away. Tanned, blond, and with one of those bodies that should never wear clothes, Jorge was a sexy sybarite. He had a great apartment that overlooked the beach, so, of course, I moved in. Jorge was a bit older, but I never asked his age. He didn't tell me much about himself except that he had a Mexican mother and a German father and he was born in Mexico. Sex with Jorge was like the local marijuana. So strong, a few hits and you were high all day. Jorge made love like he was dancing the samba and his lusty thrusting left me weak. After making sure I was satisfied, Jorge would jump out of bed and cook us a meal. I would stay in bed and smoke pot while he danced naked around the tiny kitchen. In the afternoons, I would go to a little bakery under the apartment building, where I could satisfy my "munchies". At night, if we weren't out with some tourist, we usually went to a club called Boccacio's. We drank champagne and made out while we danced under the disco ball.

Jorge always treated me like a princess but I knew we weren't in love. I didn't want to be with him, I wanted to *be* him. I wanted to live like he did, seemingly without having to work. I couldn't figure out how did it. After a couple of weeks I finally realized that Jorge was a part-time waiter and a part-time gigolo. I didn't have a problem with it. I still wanted to be him, but without the sex for money part. One morning we were having breakfast listening to his

Sergio Mendes and Brasil 66's in-concert album. I got courageous and told Jorge that I wanted to stay in Acapulco and live like he did. He smiled and raised his eyebrows. Then I pointedly added, "Without the sex." Jorge laughed and said he was sure I could charm my way into or out of anything. He told me I should come with him to one of the hotels and watch him in action.

We put on our bathing suits and took a taxi to the Hyatt Regency. After splitting up in the lobby, I took a seat at the bar and watched Jorge stroll casually out to the pool. He grabbed a towel from the pool boy's cart and selected a lounge chair next to three women. Ten minutes later one of the women took Jorge to the bar and bought him a drink. He lit her cigarette and after about five minutes the woman got up and walked through the lobby to the elevator. Five minutes later Jorge followed. Thirty minutes later, I was still sitting in the lobby when the elevator door opened and I saw Jorge with his arm around a giggling maid. He winked at me as he walked by on his way to the pool to find another willing woman.

I was exhausted just watching so I made my way down to the beach. I chose a lounge chair near an American couple. I could tell they had just arrived. They had pale white skin and I could see the beginning of a bad sunburn. They were about to naively pay a beach vender way too much for some jewelry, so I decided to go for it.

"They expect you to barter," I said.

I made sure they paid only a little too much for the souvenirs and they were happy to accept my help. We introduced ourselves and they started asking me questions about everything tourist. I told them what not to eat, where they should go for dinner, what not to miss, and so on. They had plenty of vacation money and spent it all afternoon. The husband ordered three dangerous "coco locos". I wisely sipped mine slowly but they slurped theirs right down. Soon they were tipsy and laughing over the stories about their cab driver getting lost. As the sun started to set, I got up to leave and they invited me to join them for dinner. They just assumed I too was a guest at the hotel so I went along with it. We agreed to meet in an hour and as they went to their room to change I went into the lobby's bathroom. I had my only sundress rolled up in my purse and put it on over my bathing suit.

I waited at the bar with a fresh drink in hand and when my sunburned couple showed up I asked for the check. I pretended I was looking for my room key so I could charge it to my room and, just as I hoped, the man slapped a twenty-dollar bill on the bar and said, "Let's go." We had a wonderful dinner at Jorge's restaurant, Blackbeard's, and when he saw us sitting so cozy in a booth he smiled and winked at me. He seemed proud.

I started to do this easy arrangement most every day and I met a lot of Americans who loved to spend money.

The more adventurous ones I took to places like Armando's Le Club in Old Acapulco. Everyone knew me there and I felt like I belonged in this exotic beach town.

One day I was relaxing in a beach lounge chair, watching the Acapulco Princess Hotel being built. I decided I would live here forever.

That was my last day in Acapulco.

When I went home that night Jorge told me he got a phone call while he was working at Blackbeard's. "It was your dad," he said. "He thinks you're in a Mexican prison for being a drug dealer."

I laughed but Jorge was serious. I got to a phone and called my really freaked out parents.

"Thank God you wrote and told us the name of the restaurant where your friend works!" my mother shrieked into the phone. "Your father was ready to get on a plane."

"Put Dad on the phone, please," I said with a fake smile.

My dad explained that he got a phone call from a girl who wouldn't tell them her name. She told them I was being held in a Mexican prison for dealing drugs and they would never see me again. Then she hung up the phone. I tried to laugh it off as I attempted to figure out who wanted to hurt me so badly. Suddenly I was negotiating with my parents for more time before I left Mexico, which they were begging me to do. I agreed to start the paperwork for my exit visa and promised to get in touch with my sister who was living in Los Angeles. They seemed relieved when I agreed to stay with her for at least two weeks, but I figured I'd bail after about ten days.

Like most siblings, my sister and I were very different people. I was mellow, too much so at times, and had an easygoing personality even as a child. My sister, who was one month shy of two years younger, suffered from manic depressive behavior for as long as I could remember. Everything was difficult for my sister and it was exhausting to be around her. In 1974 my parents and I were still in the dark about how to help her. We "walked on eggshells" whenever my sister was around, and the tension was palpable. We always thought she was going through a tough patch or a rough phase, but deep down we knew we were kidding ourselves. My mother believed all we needed was to be loved and well fed and we would "turn out" all right. My sister, even though she was pretty and smart, was also self-destructive and had several suicidal episodes. When she was having a bad summer in her crummy little Atlantic City apartment, she would take sleeping pills— Tuinals aka "Christmas trees" or Seconal, which we called "reds"—and get on a bus for Levittown. By the time she got home to my parents she was semiconscious and my dad would have to walk her around the house until she could stand up in the shower. And it was getting worse instead of better. I didn't know what to expect when I saw her again..

Everything moved so slowly in Mexico that it took two weeks before I could get a visa to leave the country. By then, my sister had moved from Los Angeles to Las Vegas. It didn't matter to me. I put on my only sundress dress and my espadrilles, packed my one suitcase, and got into a taxi. I couldn't believe I just said goodbye to Jorge and Acapulco. As the plane took off, I closed my eyes and tried to remember where I'd left the rest of my stuff. As soon as I was able to return to Mexico, I promised myself, I would get my photos of Bruce Springsteen and my favorite clothes from Billy's parent's house. Then I would spend the rest of my days on a lounge chair by the beautiful *Bahia de Acapulco* (Bay of Acapulco)..

4

My sister and her boyfriend met my plane in Las Vegas and we drove to Caesars Palace where I stood at the craps table for the next six hours.

Then I stayed in Las Vegas for three months.

I don't know what it was exactly that made me want to scream "Mexico Schmexico!" but I'll try to explain what attracted me to such a wasteland. There's something hypnotic about bells ringing all the time mixed with the chirpy sounds of slot machines and people shooting craps. Plus the drinks were free and everything was shiny and clean and lit up twenty-four hours a day.

It was August 1974 and the Mob ran Las Vegas. It was a lot like the movie *Casino*, a dangerous and exciting place to be. My sister had also stayed a lot longer than she planned after she met the guy who ran the Sunday brunch at Caesars Palace. Even though we had no money and no jobs, we always had a fridge full of lunchmeat and little pastries. My sister and I were getting along better than ever and having fun in a perverse way. Las Vegas suited my sister's personality. She loved cheap, flashy, shiny things, so this place was her "Cholula". The energy in the casinos was infectious and money was literally falling on the floor in front of me. I had left "love in the time of Cholula" and fallen down the rabbit hole. On any given night the biggest stars in the world played the casino showrooms: Frank Sinatra, Liza Minnelli, Liberace and, yes, even Elvis. Mort Sahl and B.B. King were frequent lounge acts.

Even though it was "Sin City", my sister and I tried to lead somewhat normal lives. I met Richard, the tennis pro at the MGM Grand, and we never went out to the casinos, just stayed home and had sex. The son of tennis great "Pancho" Gonzalez, was very handsome and one of his thighs was much bigger than the other. Richard knew how to use that leg muscle during sex. I don't know exactly what he was doing but it felt amazing. I liked Richard but he worked all day giving private tennis lessons to rich women. Eventually I got tired of waiting around at the MGM pool for a half hour of sex in the cabana and let him go. My sister was only twenty years old, and too young to work, but I got hired as a photographer in the Buddy Hackett Showroom at the Sahara Hotel. My hours were from 9 P.M. to 2 A.M. I hung out in the dressing room where the topless show girls were getting partially dressed. I had a ridiculously skimpy outfit complete with a push up bra, seamed stockings, and silver shoes. Every night I tried to sell my badly shot black-and-white pictures to people who didn't want them. The quota was two hundred fifty dollars, so I never made any money and I quit after two weeks. There had to be an easier way to make a little rent money.

My sister's boyfriend could get us into the pool area at Caesars Palace so we had somewhere to go every day. One afternoon, after turning down a half dozen requests to join various men for some "fun", my sister and I decided to do what any girl who wouldn't have sex for money does. We decided to "hustle" chips to pay the rent. I used all the techniques I learned from Jorge in Acapulco and it was really easy to do. We'd sleep until noon, show up at the casino about 3 P.M., and zoom in on the tourists who had a little too much to drink. Not drunk, just a little light headed. Las Vegas visitors were typically on a three-day "junket". They arrived on Sunday and left on Wednesday. A new group arrived on Thursday and left on Saturday. If we stayed on a three-hotel rotation, we could avoid running into the same guys more than once.

The unsuspecting, mostly Canadian, tourists we met assumed we were also on a "junket", and not living in a $185/month one-bedroom in the Enchanted Garden apartment complex. By 5 P.M. we were in a casino at the craps table with our first junket men of the night. After they started drinking way too much we'd do whatever we could to distract them. "Look, there's Liza!" I've been known to say while pocketing a couple of chips. By 7 P.M. we'd excuse ourselves and head to the bathroom where we'd change out of our standard outfit of short shorts, a tube top (bathing suit underneath), high heels, and sometimes a towel tied as a turban on our heads, and into dresses that were rolled up in our giant purses. We'd take the chips we had stuck all over us and in our bathing suit tops and cash them in on our way out. Then we'd jump into a taxi and head to the second casino and find a fresh set of marks. We only bothered with Caesars Palace, the Hilton, and the new MGM Grand. We wouldn't be caught dead downtown because we didn't have to. This place was easier to maneuver than Acapulco. We could make the rent money in a couple of hours.

When we met men we could stand to be with for more than an hour, we'd let them take us to expensive dinners and shows. We saw Frank Sinatra at Caesars Palace twice. Grown men from New Jersey cried when he sang "My Way". We were living like we were on vacation and never paid for anything. On the rare night we stayed home or got home early, my sister and I would watch TV. We got all dressed up to watch Rhoda's wedding and I stayed up late to watch *The Tomorrow Show* hosted by Tom Snyder.

My parents were ecstatic that their two daughters were living together. They didn't seem to care that Las Vegas was no place for two girls in their twenties. I didn't know what the hell I was doing in Las Vegas. Spending every day at the casino while wearing one of three rotating dresses got old very fast. Sleeping in until at least noon and then staying up until at least 2 AM every night got tiresome too. Living in one hundred degrees heat was stifling. And if I saw one more pasty white clueless tourist I was going to lose it. After three months, my sister and I decided it was time to get the hell out of there and go back home to Levittown. We chose to tell my parents in a letter written on "borrowed" Caesars Palace stationery. My parents should have written this letter *to us*, but they never did. That tells you all you need to know.

My sister wrote first.

Dear Mom & Dad,

We think we should come home and get ourselves together. We just don't see any need to be so far from you two, and we also miss our friends. We feel we are both ready to find a career. We're ready to find some field we're each interested in and get an occupation. We may move to New York, but never this far away again. We miss you. So we are planning on coming home around November 1. I've been considering the interior decorating field and Anita hasn't decided yet. Maybe in a few months I'll get an apartment in Philadelphia. Anita just remembered her field cosmetic representative. Anita and I met some guys today at the pool and we're going out to dinner soon, so I can't write real long. Now Anita wants to write something.

Hi. I got my hair cut and it's shaped around my face. I'm glad you liked the Sinatra medallion. We miss you.

Love, A & A

I would have preferred going back to Mexico but I was fine with moving home for a little while. I would gladly let my mother feed me until I burst. I would have my own bedroom. I would have a car to drive. It would be good for my sister too. After three months in Vegas, we would be grateful for our simple middle class suburban lives.

5

On July 13, 1975 my sister died at the Jersey Shore after ingesting a combination of liquid Methadone and scotch. She went to bed and never woke up. That was the day I broke up with God. I never even said goodbye to Jesus. I don't remember much about the next six months. Somehow my shattered parents went back to their jobs, and I, you guessed it, got a waitress job in New Hope.

During my drive on Interstate 95 I searched the radio for the saddest song I could find. Crying while driving, especially if it was raining was a great release for me. It was better than being numb all the time. That's why I started to love sad songs—the sadder the better. Here's a list of some of my favorites in case you ever need it:

"So Long Marianne" by Leonard Cohen

"In the Shape of a Heart" by Jackson Browne

"Wild Horses" by the Rolling Stones

"Anyone Who Had a Heart" by Dusty Springfield

"Walk on By" by Dionne Warwick

"Birds" by Neil Young

"Broken Arrow" by Buffalo Springfield

"The River" and "Downbound Train" by Bruce
Springsteen

"To Love Somebody" by The Bee Gees

"Love Has No Pride" by J.D. Souther

During the months after my sister's death, music became my therapy. There was no Dr. Phil but I did have Dr. Wu. I played Steely Dan's *Katy Lied* album over and over, trying to figure out what the hell it was about. Even without having a clue about what they meant, the words to those songs spoke to me. (They remain just as mysterious and even profound today. I recently Googled the lyrics and found out about the katydid on the cover. Funny, I never noticed the cover before.)

One of my sister's friends mercifully came to Levittown to visit. She invited me to go into Center City Philadelphia with her to have dinner. First we stopped at the American Academy of Broadcasting on Chestnut Street so she could check out a school for TV newscasters. She was very pretty and perfect for the job but she wrong about the class. A few minutes into a hilarious pitch by a local radio personality named Bob Gale, I realized we were at a school for wannabe DJs. I don't know how or why it happened, but something made me think *I* should do this. I went home and told my parents about my new dream. There was no response until I mentioned the price of tuition. My dad wasn't interested in expensive things, or how much something cost. If you wanted to impress him, reveal *how little* you paid for it. When I announced that five hundred dollars was all I needed to live my dream my dad was suddenly very happy for me. He gave me the check and I signed up for weekly classes.

The American Academy of Broadcasting was owned by Philadelphia's own "boss jock", "Long John Wade". I drove in from my parent's house every Saturday, and sometimes on Wednesdays, in my Toyota Corolla. I learned how to read a commercial and how to lose my Philly accent. Six weeks later I "graduated" and was instructed to "knock on every door of every radio station in town and never take no for an answer." I didn't know enough to be discouraged. One night I called the request line of WMMR, my favorite radio station. After about two hundred rings, the DJ himself, Steve Martorano, answered. I started to blurt out my story and was telling him how I could drive in from Levittown anytime when I heard Steve trying to interrupt me.

"What do you look like?" he asked.

I giggled and said something that he must have liked. Steve told me to drive to 19th and Walnut Streets and stop in front of the station at 10 P.M. He said he'd be standing on the corner and if I liked what I saw I should pull over. When I hung up the phone I almost fainted and when I saw Steve standing in front of the Wellington Building later that evening I almost fainted again. I thought he looked like Al Pacino from the movie *Serpico*, so I pulled over and he got in the car. Steve told me to drive around Rittenhouse Square. He pointed to a parking space and I pulled over. After we fogged up the car windows, Steve said he was in a hurry to go somewhere and asked if I wanted to meet him at WMMR on Saturday night. I just nodded as Steve got out of the car and disappeared into the night. That's how I became an "intern" at WMMR.

Those were the days when DJs got to pick the music they played from a library of albums chosen at weekly music meetings. As the new albums were released, the Music Director of the radio station and all the DJs voted on which songs to add. Each DJ arrived about a half hour before their shift and chose the first hour of music. To avoid repeating a song or artist, the previous DJ always pulled the album covers about halfway out of the shelf. That's how you knew who played what. The time and date it was played, plus the DJs initials, were written on the cover. The music you played could be influenced by the day's events, or what was going on in your personal life, or just be your new favorite song. You could even play a request every once in a while. Sometimes I would only plan one song ahead and just let the music tell me what to play next. Creating sets of music with great segues from one song to another used to be what made a great DJ.

This was before the dreaded three C's of radio: consultants, charts, and categories. Program directors were often fired when the ratings for the radio station didn't generate enough sales revenue. Instead of always being the one to take the blame, program directors started to hire consultants. They could be anyone—a former program director, a good salesman with a limited background in music, or someone who was getting paid or had some sort of personal interest in certain bands or record labels—as long as they were male. Some were better than others at predicting what should be on a radio station's playlist. It's a lot like psychics. Some guess right some of the time. The problem is each city is different. You have to live there to know what's going on. The consultant would make up categories for the music based on tempo, length, or the year it was recorded. Each category was assigned a letter of the alphabet. The consultant would create a "hot clock", which was a pie chart that represented an hour of music. Most of the music was removed from the library and only the songs the consultant approved of remained in the studio. In some cases the number of available music went from thousands to hundreds.

Someone had the bright idea to "day-part" certain songs. The consultant or program director decided which songs were too loud and only allowed them to be played at certain hours of the day. Before each shift the DJ would look at the "hot clock", note the next card in that category, and play the song. You could not deviate from the plan. If things went badly the program director could convince the general manager that it was the fault of the consultant. This would give him at least six more weeks to get another job and put his big house up for sale. Thankfully when I started my radio career, the DJs still had the power.

When I met Steve Martorano I not only got a job in radio, I thought I had met my new love. Steve was funny, smart, glib, and hip and he knew I had a big crush on him. I thought we were perfect for each other. After Steve's show on Saturday nights, we would go to a local bar called Doobie's on 22nd and Lombard Street. Steve introduced me to all the other DJs, the record promoters, and I met the local musicians who played there. Some great bands come from Philadelphia, South Jersey, and Delaware. We had The Hooters, Robert Hazard and the Heroes, The A's, Beru Revue, Tommy Conwell and the Young Rumblers, and Kenn Kweder and his Secret Kidds.

I met Bobbi Silver for the first time at Doobies's.

Philly had some colorful and crazy record promoters like Mattie "the Humdinger" Singer, WDAS's "Butterball";s brother Richie Tamburro, and the original wild and crazy guy, John Betancourt. But the best of them all was Bobbi Silver. Bobbi retired in 2011 after forty-two years doing promotion for record labels. She's one of a kind, a trailblazer and record breaker in every sense of the word. A long list of superstars, including Sting, Lady Gaga, 50 Cent and Beck, will tell you how much they dig Bobbi.

Bobbi started her career in the record business in 1969 as a secretary at Jamie's Records on North Broad Street in Philadelphia. When their promotion guy was fired, Bobbi stepped in. She showed up at the radio stations without first revealing that she was a girl. After a few awkward moments, it was clear Bobbi had found her niche. Bobbi Silver would do this for the next forty-two years. Every single day she was prepared and committed. Bobbi never let up and never let anyone down. Her reputation grew as someone who would do anything to get the record played. Bobbi was hired by some of the "heavies" of the record business: Chris Blackwell, who founded Island Records; Neil Bogart, who started Casablanca Records; and in 1973 she was working for RSO Records with Robert Stigwood at the helm. Michael McKean and David L. Lander, who played "Lenny" and "Squiggy" on the TV show *Laverne and Shirley*, released a comedy album on Casablanca Records. When Michael McKean was later cast in the movie *This Is Spinal Tap*, he reportedly started calling Fran Drescher's record promoter character "Bobbi" during rehearsals, in homage to Bobbi Silver. According to rock 'n' roll legend, that's how the character "Bobbi Flekman" was born.

While most people wished they had the balls to do things that were dangerous and daring, Bobbi did these things every day. She dressed like a rock star in fringed leather. Bobbi had beautiful necklaces made with tiny silver spoons. The cocaine vials she carried were encrusted in jewels. Her apartment was filled with sculpture and paintings and lots of antiques. The large white table at Bobbi's was the coolest place to be. If you were lucky enough to be included in the group of crazies who sat at that table, you had made it. Whenever she left to go to a record convention and had to stay overnight, Bobbi always put three things in her suitcase: a pair of socks with tons of cash rolled up inside, a roll of aluminum foil, and a scale.

One night we were on the train on our way back to Philly from New York. The trip took about an hour and a half. Sleep deprived and strung out, Bobbi and I took turns going to the bathroom to do a couple of lines of cocaine. I was waiting for her to come back to our seats and toss me the vial for what seemed like a long time. Then I saw her with a crazy grin on her face. Bobbi was walking down the aisle of the train laughing hysterically. One of her arms was stained blue from her fingers to her elbows.

"Guess what fell in the toilet?" she said.

How could I not love this woman?

From Rick Springfield to 50 Cent, Bobbi Silver

was always on the job.

6

I knew Steve Martorano liked me, but he had a girlfriend

and he *loved* her. Before I finally figured that out I showed

up at the radio station every week after my broadcasting

class. One Saturday night I was at WMMR in the studio

with Steve and he played a song from a new album by

Warren Zevon. I was so focused on Steve I wasn't even

listening to the song. Warren was in town that night at The

Main Point and I thought I could talk Steve into taking me.

He laughed and said I should go by myself and instead of

getting angry and going home to be miserable, I got angry

and went to The Main Point. Before then, I had never heard

of Warren and don't know what it was that made me go.

On June 19, 1976, I took the only empty seat right

in front of the stage and five minutes after he hesitantly

took a seat behind the piano, I was insanely attracted to Warren Zevon. Although he was dressed in a very nice suit, he didn't seem to care about how disheveled he looked. His songs were sad, funny, and what I considered very "L.A.", like songs the Eagles would have written if they were bipolar. I wanted to stay for the second show and was about to go to the bathroom and hide until the crowd left when Warren suddenly appeared in front of me.

"Did you like the show?" he asked in a very loud and deep voice, while smiling a little too much.

"Yes," I said. "I was going to stay for the second show but…"

I was suddenly distracted by a girl walking toward us with a mean look on her face.

"Give me a minute," Warren snapped at her. After the girl walked away he said, "Why don't you come back tomorrow night?"

"Is she with you?" I said, pointing to the girl with my chin.

"She's leaving," he answered, giving me a strained, crazy smile. "I met her last night in Jersey after I wrote a song with Bruce Springsteen." Warren grinned again, obviously pleased with the opportunity to name drop.

"I think I should go," I said, secretly hoping Warren would object.

"Yeah, okay. But come back tomorrow and make sure you let me know when you get here." Warren smiled, his eyes darting around the room.

"Okay, I'll see you then" I replied and started for the door. Warren didn't stop me so I drove home. I was up all night thinking about what it would be like to see him again.

I returned to the club the next night. I was a little too nervous to barge into the backstage area so I took a seat in the audience. I thought I saw the girl from Freehold. If she was there, by the time the show was over, she was gone. After the show, I went to Warren's small dressing room and knocked on the door. He seemed surprised to see me. We shared an awkward hug and then sat down on a small sofa. We couldn't get close enough to each other. He had a drink in a paper cup and I know it's supposed to be odorless but I smelled vodka. I leaned into him and his skin felt hot and I don't know what made me do it but I slipped my hand into his pocket. At that moment photographer Phil Ceccola shot some pictures of us. Years later, Phil gave me the contact sheet. Those first night photos of Warren and I are some of my all time favorites.

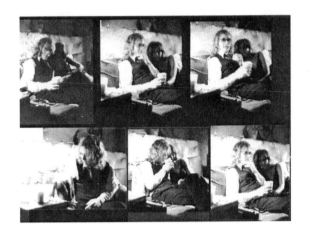

We stayed up all night in Warren's hotel room. It was almost too much for me to handle. The first time we had sex I couldn't breathe. My heart was racing and tried to calm down but I couldn't be the cool girl who did this kind of thing all the time. I was trembling when Warren took my clothes off and then just stood and looked at me on the bed. He removed his suit and sat next to me on the bed. He pushed me down and started to kiss me. Warren took his time, which whipped me into a frenzy. I was like the crazed, horny version of myself. I silently hoped Warren wouldn't expect this all the time. I knew the real me was going to emerge sooner than later. I couldn't really be this much in love with a guy I just met. But for some reason the tryst felt like something deep.

After we stopped mauling each other, we fell asleep. In the morning over breakfast, in a calm voice, Warren told me all about his marriage, wife, and baby. He said he wanted me to know the truth and I thanked him for being honest. I thought the next conversation would be about how we couldn't see each other again. Instead, he asked me to come to Boston, where he had a day off before his next show, and I was thrilled. It made it a lot easier to leave Warren, knowing I would see him again. I went home, packed a bag and the next day I was on a flight to Boston. I took a taxi to the Lennox Hotel on Boyleston Street. Warren was very happy to see me and seemed relieved that he wasn't alone anymore. We stayed in bed and only left the room to catch a Toots and the Maytals show. We laughed a lot and couldn't get enough of each other. When it was time for me to leave, Warren told me he'd stay in touch but I didn't think I would hear from him again.

I was wrong.

A couple of months later Warren called when he came to Philly with his record promoter Burt Stein. Warren and Burt checked into hotels as "Starsky and Hutch". I was working as a hostess at a nearby restaurant called The Fish Market with a girl who had a crush on Burt. After work, we went to the Latham Hotel on 17th Street. I had another ridiculously great time. Warren was funny, crazy, and wild. He looked me in the eyes like he was trying to read my mind. I wanted to tell him I'd lost it months ago. Then he kissed me and I melted into his arms. The hours went by too quickly and it was becoming more difficult to say goodbye.

In October Steve Martorano got a phone call from his friend Roy Perry. Roy was the new program director at

WCAU FM. The station replaced its "oldies" format with a blend of disco and R&B music. Roy asked Steve if he knew anyone who could do some weekend shifts and Steve recommended me. Steve not only helped me make an audition tape, he was finally able to prove to his girlfriend that he really was trying to get me a job. With my audition tape in hand, I drove over to the station in Bala Cynwyd and dropped it off.

It took two days before I received the call. R.J. Laurence, the program director, told me I got the job. I was trembling as I drove to the radio station and tried to keep my cool when I was told how much money I would make. I couldn't believe it was really happening to me. According to my 1968 Social Security statement, I earned $59. It went up to $762 in 1969. In 1976 I earned $1,549. The next year—my first year in radio—I made $12,285.00. For a former hostess, the jump was palpable.

As much as I loved my new job as a DJ, the hours were brutal. I was up at 4:30 A.M. and back at home by 11 A.M. I didn't know what to do all day. I had to have dinner by six and I was in bed by nine. If I went to a concert I ended up staying up all night and paid the price the next day. Sleep deprivation and too much cocaine turned me into a different girl than the one that got hired. I wasn't the fun, stay up late girl anymore.

At the end of my four hours on the radio, I was suddenly alone. I wasn't lonely, but I felt so connected to the listeners and the music, it was too quiet and dull when I went home. Going from the high of being on the radio to anything ordinary was tough. Most days after my show I would call Bobbi Silver and she would let me go with her to the radio stations to promote her newest hits. I was just trying to have a little daytime fun but being Bobbi Silver's friend gave me instant credibility in the music world.

Bobbi and I would get into her big black car and take the Pennsylvania Turnpike to Harrisburg or Allentown. Bobbi knew *everything* about each program director—their birthday, wife's name, where they worked before, and when they liked her to call them every week. She never missed one call or was a minute late. Once a week Bobbi drove over the bridge to New Jersey to see Kal Rudman. One day I went along and I was shocked when I met this man who looked like he could be my uncle "bopping" around his office with music blaring. Kal Rudman is the founder and publisher of *Friday Morning Quarterback* (better known as *FMQB*), *the* trade magazine of the radio and music industries. Kal had a modest office in Cherry Hill, New Jersey. Bill Hard wrote his tip sheet for rock radio stations, picking the songs he believed deserved to be added to a radio station's playlist and—equally important—the number of times (spins) a song was played each day after it was placed in rotation. Both men were generous and kind to me and I started co-writing a column in Kal's tip sheet with Roy Perry. The column was national, which made me known to program and music directors all over the country. I'm sure my good fortune was only because I showed up with Bobbi Silver

I was very excited when Bobbi invited me to the opening of a new disco called Xenon in New York. It would become the only real rival of Studio 54. On June 24, 1978 Bobbi and I were about to leave a Bobby Poe record convention in Washington, D.C and fly to New York but we hadn't slept in three days so Bobbi decided not to go. I made the trip anyway, with Al Coury, the co-founder of RSO Records. Al is legendary. In 1970 Al was vice president of Capital Records where he worked since 1957. He persuaded Paul McCartney to include the song "Helen Wheels" on the U.S. version of *Band on the Run*. John Lennon asked him to work his studio magic just like he had for the careers of the Beach Boys, Pink Floyd, Bob Seeger, and Linda Ronstadt. Al chose the song "Whatever Gets You Through the Night" for Lennon's *Walls and Bridges* album. My favorite story is when John Lennon asked Al to retrieve the master tapes of *Rock 'n' Roll* from trigger happy, crazy but brilliant producer Phil Spector. And, of course, Al did it.

Al and I flew to New York together directly from the record convention and checked into the Sherry Netherland Hotel on 781 5th Avenue. Al got me my own room and it was exquisite. Even the toilet was beautifully decorated. After dinner, we took a money green limo to Xenon on 124 West 43rd Street and met the Bee Gees, who were sitting in a booth with their mother. We drank champagne and watched half naked people go-go dancing to the Bee Gees' music. It was wonderfully surreal.

Late one night I answered the phone and it was Warren calling from Hawaii. Warren could always get my phone number from someone in the radio or record business. I was surprised and thrilled to hear his voice. He told me he'd written a song called "Lawyers, Guns and Money". He explained that he was vacationing with Burt Stein, his record promoter, because Joe Smith, the president of the record label, thought Warren needed a little break. "Listen to this," he said as he started singing this song about Honduras and waitresses and Russians. After he sang the last line, Warren asked me what I thought.

"Do you think they'll play it on the radio with the word 'shit' in it?" I asked.

"Oh they'll play it," Warren said and then he laughed a little too hard.

What I didn't know at the time was that Warren needed a little break from breaking things. Like the banister in his rented house after a night of heavy drinking. Warren's wife Crystal called his pal Jackson Browne, took the baby, and split. Jackson came over to check on Warren and they wrote "Tenderness on the Block". Warren didn't seem to remember doing anything violent and no one ever discussed what exactly happened to the banister. Warren's wife said in an interview that it was Jackson, not Joe Smith, who suggested that Burt Stein take Warren to Hawaii. Either way, it says a lot about how a whole bunch of people could be clueless about how to help someone they loved.

I don't know if Warren was trying to force his wife to leave him, but it sure seemed that way to me. When Warren called me to be sure I'd be at his show at the Bijou Café on March 6, 1978, he said he told his wife about me and insisted that she and I have dinner together. When I met Crystal she seemed sweet and was quiet and soft spoken. Warren gave her his credit card and she and I went to a restaurant and ate snails. I asked her why she was having dinner with me and she tried to explain that Warren had to feel like a rock star and had trouble living a routine married life. She blamed it on his drinking problem. I didn't believe that she believed a word of what she was saying. I went back to the hotel with her and when Warren joined us I could see the panic in her eyes. She knew he wanted us all to jump into bed together but it was the last thing she wanted. Just when I thought it couldn't get any more awkward, their baby started crying in the adjoining room. Even though they had brought along their own au pair, Warren's wife ran into the baby's room and I got out of there as fast as I could and went home.

After the "botched ménage", I didn't think I'd hear from him again.

Again I was wrong.

The next time Warren called me was in March 1978 and he put his wife on the phone. She said a couple of words in a faraway voice before handing the phone back to Warren. He said I should come to L.A. and visit them. I know it sounds as if I had lost my mind but I decided to take him up on his offer. In some sort of twisted way I was flattered. I planned a trip to visit my friends director Steve Rash and producer Fred Bauer who with their wives were living large in Malibu. They were literally living their dream, making a movie about Buddy Holly called *The Buddy Holly Story*. The screenplay was written by Robert Gittler, a.k.a. Robert Gale. Coincidentally, he was the same guy who taught that first class I stumbled into at the American Academy of Broadcasting. Steve and Fred rented houses right on the beach in the Malibu Colony, just a few doors down from Linda Ronstadt's house and right next door to Michael Landon.

After a couple of crazy days hanging out on the set in Culver City I knew what I had to do. Against my better judgment I decided to drop in on Warren. I persuaded my friend Jay to drive me to Griffith Park. I looked up the address in a *Thomas Guide* and we got on the 134 Freeway and headed east. When we arrived at the two-story house, I got out of the car. I made Jay drive away before I knocked on the door. I knew it was a crazy move but I had to see for myself what was going on with Warren and his wife.

Warren finally answered the door wearing a bathrobe with a drink in one hand and a .357 magnum in the other. It was the first time I witnessed how drunk he could get. I could feel the tension in the house before I even walked inside. Warren barely said hello to me. Instead he started yelling about being described as "pudgy" in a review of his most recent concert. Then he turned to me and smiled and said, "How ya' doin?" I laughed nervously and followed him into the living room. Crystal came out of the kitchen and gave me a frosty hello. I grunted back. I sat on the couch and Warren sat on the bench of a piano that was too big for the room. He started to play something when his wife announced "Dinner's ready."

I followed Warren into the dining room, sat at the table, and waited to see what would happen next. His wife put the food on the table and walked back into the kitchen. I was sure it had poison in it but I tried to eat something anyway. After twenty excruciating minutes, Warren pushed away his plate. "We're going to the movies," he sneered at his wife and I clearly sensed she wasn't invited. Relieved to be leaving, I popped a Quaalude and welcomed the near-instant way it made me feel. I staggered into a car and someone drove Warren and I to the movies to see *The Fury*. I passed out during the first five minutes, until I heard Warren yelling. He was elbowing me in the ribs. I tried to make out what he was saying.

"What?" I finally asked.

"Listen," Warren yelled.

"What?" I asked again.

"What are they all saying?" Warren yelled again.

I then heard the audience yelling something that sounded like "bogus".

Warren couldn't stand it anymore and he stood up and screamed, "What are you people yelling?"

"*Focus!*" someone yelled back. "The picture is out of focus."

Warren took my hand and pulled me out of my seat. We spilled into a taxi and went back to Los Feliz.

Back at "Casa Crazy", Burt Stein, the record promoter from Warren's record label, was sitting in the living room. He was talking to Warren's wife about an interview for *People* magazine that was scheduled for the next day. When he suggested that I leave before the camera crew arrived, Warren got angry and there was lots of yelling and screaming. I went upstairs and saw the gun lying on his bed with the barrel open. I took out the cartridge and hid it in one of the dresser drawers. I heard glass breaking so I started to gather my stuff and tried to find a telephone. I found the phone, went into the closet, and called my friends to calmly ask them to come and pick me up. On way back downstairs I sat on the steps and waited for my ride to arrive. When the doorbell rang, Warren answered and I heard my friend Fred Bauer say, "Can Anita come out and play?"

"Sure," Warren said sarcastically as he turned to look at me. "So you're leaving?"

"Yes, I think I should go," I said nervously.

"Sure," Warren said again. "Go." Then he flashed with that eerie Jack Nicholson "*Heeere's Johnny*" smile.

I practically ran to my friend's car and we sped away. I didn't tell him what happened. I didn't think he would believe me if I told him what I had just seen.

A couple of months later, I read the *People* magazine article. In the May 22, 1978 issue Sue Reilly wrote an article called ROCKED L.A.; IT'S THE EXCITABLE WARREN ZEVON:

> "The boozy poet of weirdo
> rock," says his drummer,
> "is really a giant lamb."
>
> L.A.'s newest
> darling desperado, Warren
> Zevon, likes to start his
> day with a screwdriver,
> then clear his head with
> coffee and a side of vodka,
> and eventually escalate to

vodka and coffee, hold the coffee. About a bottle of Stolichnaya down the road, Zevon is ready to go to work. "I used to get a lot of drunk driving tickets," he admits, "so I knew it would come down to drinking or driving. I don't drive anymore."

Warren himself allows that after his first success, "I got a little crazy," and briefly separated from his wife Crystal and their daughter Ariel, now almost 2.

"Warren was trying to adjust to being famous," Crystal says understandingly. "He needed to go out and be single and find out that fame doesn't take the place of a family." When he came back 3 months later, she reports, "He was a different man. I couldn't ask for a kinder, more involved husband." As for the Stolichnaya curtain, she says, "I treat Warren the same as anyone with a drinking problem. I give him space to work it out."

Zevon married Crystal,
now 28, after driving all
night to a wedding chapel
in Vegas. Warren has a
son, Jordan, 8, whom he
regularly visits, from a brief
first marriage. Even with
his new acclaim, Zevon
still plays on a rented
piano in a modest rented
home.

After I read the article I tossed the magazine in the garbage and tried to forget about Warren. He was crazy and I decided never to see him again. But as I would find out, Warren wasn't prepared to let me go.

7

In August 1978 Warren phoned to say he was getting a divorce. He sounded surprisingly sober. When I heard Warren's voice I realized how much I missed him. I couldn't stop smiling and he kept talking about me visiting him in his apartment on the Sunset Strip. I thought of his song called "Join Me in L.A." in which Warren sings about calling somebody long distance and asking them to, well, join him in L.A.

"So what you're saying is, you want me to *join you in L.A.?*" I asked, hoping Warren would notice that I knew the song.

"Yes," he whispered and just like that, once again, I was hooked.

I *was* planning on attending a cousin's Bar Mitzvah in northern California. I told Warren I'd stop in L.A. on my way back to Philly and spend a few days with him. But then I had to get back to my radio job.

"Can't you pre-tape it?" Warren asked, pretending not to know better.

"No, but we'll have a few days together," I said breathlessly. I was shaking. What was it about this guy that made me forget everything else?

A couple of weeks later I arrived at Warren's Sunset Boulevard apartment. He was on the phone when he answered the door. He waved me in and then started vacuuming the rug while he screamed over the roar into the phone. Finally, the chaos stopped and Warren hugged me. "Welcome," he said with a broad smile. "I just had to tidy up. It looked like that scene from *A Bridge Too Far* in here."

Those were the last words we spoke for a couple of hours. We tore our clothes off and got down on the living room floor. One of Warren's hands pulled my hair as the other went directly to a place I didn't know it could go. Later, after a short post sex nap, Warren wanted to go to L.A.'s Venice neighborhood, where his pal, Waddy Wachtel, lived. Warren had a big old beat-up blue car. I couldn't identify the make or model. He wasn't the best driver but I was on such a high of happiness I really couldn't tell how bad he was.

Waddy looked very surprised when Warren pulled up behind the wheel. I laughed along with everyone else but I started to wonder what was up with the driving thing. We scored some pot and hit the road. Warren next wanted me to meet George Gruel, his new road manager. George answered his door and hugged Warren. George was big and tall and looked like he could hurt you. Warren introduced us and then George hugged me too.

Warren put his arm around me and told George, "She loves to smoke pot and she's funny too."

"Uh-oh," George replied, lighting up a huge joint.

George and Warren shared the same odd sense of humor. They were always laughing about something that no one else quite understood.

The next day Warren drove me to The Sound Factory, the studio where he was recording *Excitable Boy*. When we arrived, Jackson Browne was standing in the parking lot and he too seemed astounded to see Warren driving. Jackson was co-producing Warren's album along with Waddy Wachtel. Jackson smiled at me as we were introduced. I tried not to gush but he was so handsome in that L.A. desperado kind of way.

Inside the studio, Jackson and I sat together at the mixing board while Warren took his place in a little vocal booth. Warren sang "Hasten Down the Wind" and

"Accidentally Like a Martyr", which Warren referred to as his divorce songs. He hit the high notes just right and Jackson was thrilled with Warren's singing. Warren decided to take a break when a tall beautiful blonde walked in. She was Jackson's girlfriend, Lynne Sweeney. They had just returned from the Running on Empty tour, where they met while Jackson was performing in Australia. They were both rock star skinny and dressed in matching blue jeans and white T-shirts. Lynne was living at Jackson's house in the hills above Hollywood. Warren introduced me to Lynne, who smiled but looked a little stressed out. As Lynne and Jackson hugged each other tightly and started kissing, Warren said, "Listen, you can hear their bones rubbing together." Everyone but Lynne laughed and then she blurted out that Warren's wife was on her way to the studio. That meant that I was on my way with Lynne to Jackson's house.

We drove through Outpost Canyon to a big house on Carmen Crest Drive. A beautiful, sprawling, rock star worthy house. There Lynne introduced me to Jackson's adorable four-year-old son, Ethan, and his nanny Elizabeth. Lynne took me on a grand tour though all the home's rooms, and seemed understandably excited about every new thing in her new life. We went into Jackson's home studio and I heard a rough cut of *Running on Empty*. Lynne clicked off the tape and whispered, "I feel so lucky."

Ethan wanted Lynne to take him out for ice cream so the three of us went to Mashti Malone's in Hollywood. I couldn't stop looking a Lynne. She was so naturally gorgeous it was hard not to stare. Jackson's son wasn't one of those monster children. He always remembered to say "please" and "thank you" and looked so cute in his T-shirt with "Nearly Famous" on the front. When we returned to the house we ditched our clothes and took a swim in Jackson's pool. I tried not to gawk when Lynne dove into the water naked and perfect. It was an idyllic afternoon. Sooner than I liked, Jackson called and said the coast was clear and Lynne drove me back to the studio.

I didn't ask Warren about the visit from his wife and he didn't talk about it. Nothing could spoil my time in L.A. with Warren. We went to the Troubadour on Santa Monica Boulevard and got drunk in the middle of the afternoon with the club's infamous owner, Doug Weston. We ate at all of Warren's favorite restaurants: Gardens of Taxco on Harper, Dan Tana's on Santa Monica, and The Musso & Frank Grill on Hollywood Boulevard.

The day I was scheduled to fly back to Philly, Jackson stopped by Warren's apartment. When Warren was in the bathroom, Jackson confided that for the past few days Warren drove and sang better than he had in months. I laughed and Jackson smiled and said, "Why don't you stick around a little longer?"

"I have a job," I answered. "And I'm not a nurse."

In October of 1978 I went to a party that changed my life. Jerry Stevens was the program director for WMMR. Jerry was known as a hard partier. In those days everyone, including your doctor, your lawyer, and most of your friends, used cocaine. A little bit was fine and really did make you look better, but in hindsight we all used way too much. Jerry Stevens was known to hire people who didn't fit the usual "disc jockey" description. He liked free spirits and people who had a passion for music as much as radio. He hired his staff from local colleges Temple and Penn State and had even hired a woman or two.

Jerry approached me at the party and whispered in my ear, "Follow me into the bathroom." While he chopped cocaine into lines for himself, he offered me a job. WMMR was the best station in town and I couldn't believe Jerry

Stevens was asking me to join the team. I would replace a girl named April and since she only used her first name, Jerry suggested that I do the same.

"April . . . Anita," he said. (snort snort) "Maybe nobody will notice the difference." (snort snort)

I was so excited, he could have asked anything of me. But, of course, it's radio, so nothing is what it seems. In the time it took to tell my friends about Jerry Stevens and his amazing offer, he was gone. Like so many program directors before him, like drummers in rock bands—they simply implode and then a new one takes his place. The new one was named Paul Fuhr. He and I had lunch and I drank too much but he hired me anyway.

On October 24, 1978, nine days after my last show on WCAU, I went on the air for the first time on WMMR. I still couldn't believe I was hosting the morning show on the biggest station in a city that at the time was the third major market. And to make the whole thing even more ridiculous, I didn't know how to use the equipment. I must have skipped the "two turntables and a microphone" class at the American Academy of Broadcasting. Thankfully Bobbi magically appeared on that first morning and rolled a joint that helped me get over my nervousness.

Against all odds, I knew just what to play and what to say to the listeners as they started their day. I had a special greeting for the Deadheads and I dubbed Van Halen "The Sweat Brothers". I had a lot of male listeners but I also had a good share of females and that was great for the sales department. My confidence and the ratings soared. I drew big crowds when I was hired to do personal appearances and live shows from shopping malls. It all seemed so easy and I was enjoying every minute of it.

On April 1, 1979, Matt Damsker's article ran in the

Philadelphia Bulletin. It was called THE SEESAW WAR FOR

TOP RADIO RATINGS and featured a photo of me with the

caption "WMMR disc jockey Anita Gevinson has a sexy vitality that makes her popular with the morning drive crowd." The only problem was that I still struggled with the early morning wake up call. I felt physically ill most every morning at 4:30 A.M. I started sleeping with "one eye open", always aware of what time it was. I never overslept but I was as sleep deprived as a first time single mom. I used to be the girl next door who was never home. Now I was the girl who was never out past nine.

To make matters worse, a third program director was brought in from the Midwest and he didn't care about me or my morning show. In fact he didn't like the show at all and we had mutual disrespect for each other. Without thinking it through, I decided to leave WMMR, the city of Philadelphia, everyone who listened to me on the radio, and my family and friends for a job in Boston, Massachusetts.

Bobbi Silver had come to my rescue three months earlier. She knew how unhappy I was toward the end at

WMMR, and so she told me to move in with her instead of renewing my apartment lease. That way I could pack up and leave in a hurry when I got my next job offer. Bobbi had moved into a two-bedroom apartment in the Warwick Hotel on 17th and Locust Streets. The hotel had a couple of floors of rental units and Bobbi lived in #911. All of the bands that came to Philadelphia stayed at the Warwick. There was a disco called Elan right off the lobby which hosted lots of drugs and dancing. At 2 A.M. the party moved up to the ninth floor to Bobbi's apartment until security banged on the door.

I found my Boston gig at one of those parties. Bobbi had invited a promo guy from Boston and the program director for the new rock station WCOZ. Before they left that night, I had a WCOZ job waiting on Stuart Street in Boston's Copley Square. The program director, a WBCN defector, was putting his air staff together. He had already hired former Philly DJ Steven Clean for the 2 P.M.

to 7 P.M. shift. The only thing I asked for was a promise that I wouldn't have to do the morning show. He said I could have the 6 P.M. to 10 P.M. shift. We had ourselves a deal.

It wasn't difficult to quit my job at WMMR because I was so mad. I was mad at my program director who I thought was ruining the radio station and making a lot of money doing it. I also found out what motivated the other radio station's "morning men" to keep those brutal hours. They were making *way* more than I was. I was the only woman in the morning and I quickly learned about the double standard that still exists today. For a while I gamely played along. I wore a vest with no shirt underneath for all of the publicity pictures. But I couldn't get past the fact that I was making less money than the men. My program director would laugh when I brought it up and never hid the fact that he felt I wasn't worth it. I knew he didn't think I'd quit my job and it was great to see the shock on his face when I did it.

I also knew deep in my soul that no one in their right mind walks away from this job.

My last show on WMMR was on April 20, 1979. Then I packed all the stuff I could fit into my Corolla and with my dad behind the wheel we hit the road. It was a mistake to leave Philly and I knew it, but it was too late. I could only hope that when I turned on the microphone at WCOZ, I would change my mind. I heard James Taylor on the radio singing about the turnpike from Stockbridge to Boston and when he got to the line "with ten miles behind me and ten thousand more to go," all I could do was cry.

8

I threw caution to the wind and decided to rent a room in my new boss's condo. Having a landlord who is also your boss isn't as dumb as it sounds; it's a lot dumber. It's not a good idea to give someone that much power. I would learn this very soon. I didn't know anyone in Boston and I didn't love anything about the place at first. I found it "too old and cold and settled in its ways," to quote a Joni Mitchell lyric, but I soon found that Boston was a great music town. It became very cool to be the new girl in town.

I tried to reinvent myself, with a new (bad) perm and a wardrobe that included hot pants and a Cub Scout shirt. I wanted to look like Linda Ronstadt did on the cover of her *Livin' in the U.S.A.* album, so I asked one of the local promo guys to buy me a pair of roller skates that outrageously cost four hundred dollars. Most afternoons I would skate up and down Beacon Street. I loved my new sleep as late as possible schedule. My room in Brookline was right across the street from the late astrologer Darrell Martinie, the "Cosmic Muffin". He did a daily horoscope report on the radio. The nickname "Cosmic Muffin" was taken from a *National Lampoon* parody and given to him by local legendary radio personality Charles Laquidara. It fit Darrell perfectly. I spent many afternoons sitting at his kitchen table drinking red wine while Darrell made delicious pasta from scratch. Tall and blond, he was usually dressed in a T-shirt, with red tights tucked into white cowboy boots. He was funny and, I believe, actually psychic. And a welcomed and wonderful new friend.

On April 23rd I did my first show on WCOZ. I wasn't an instant star like I was in Philly. I couldn't pronounce the names of the towns correctly and I don't think the listeners ever really warmed up to me. That's a bad thing in such a cold city.

Once you're part of the record and radio community, when you move from town to town, you have a built-in social network. As a DJ, I never paid for anything, including great dinners in fine restaurants and free tickets to every concert. And with my new hours I could go out and see bands at the Paradise or the Orpheum. Working from 6 P.M. to 10 P.M. also meant that I was the one who got to do a lot of interviews. Someone from one of the bands in town that night would often come to the radio station after sound check to say hello as a favor, or sometimes to try to get some "walk up" sales (last minute ticket sales) by doing an interview with me.

I was ready to meet someone new. I missed my friends from Philly and didn't feel any love from the listeners. I really needed to find something that could make me feel that way again. Warren Zevon wasn't available. Or so I thought. Just when it seemed like I would never find anyone to play with, a couple of the biggest rock stars in the world appeared at the studio door like Lenny and Squiggy from *Laverne and Shirley*. (That's not a Hall and Oates joke).

On October 26 Bob Weir stopped by WCOZ for an interview with me. He was in between Grateful Dead shows at Connecticut's New Haven Coliseum and the show at the Cape Cod Coliseum in Yarmouth. Although I knew some of the Grateful Dead's songs, I didn't really know which band member was Bob Weir. Turns out, he's the cute one. When he walked into the studio, he looked very preppy and I couldn't stop smiling at him. We were live on the air when Bob turned the tables and started asking *me* questions.

"When was your last Dead show?" Bob asked. He smiled after he said it, as if he already knew the answer.

"I've never seen a Dead show," I said really fast, feeling my credibility slip away.

"Well, we'll have to fix that, won't we?" Bob was right in my face.

He invited me to the upcoming Dead show on November 4 at the Civic Center in Providence, Rhode Island, and I had to say yes since we were live on the radio. I don't know what the hell else I said during the interview but I know I gave Bob Weir my phone number. As he was getting ready to leave, Bob hugged me tightly and said he'd call me. I went home that night and couldn't stop thinking about him. I couldn't wait to feel his hands all over my body. Bob Weir was the guest star in my sex dream that night. I doubted actual sex with Bob could be any better, so I was kind of hoping he didn't call.

A couple of days later I heard my boss answer the phone and say, "Anita, it's Bobby."

I grabbed the phone out of his hand and said "Hey, what's up?"

To my surprise, a man answered and said, "Nothing. What's up with you?" It took me a second to realize that it was Bob Weir, not Bobbi Silver. Bobby told me to meet him at the side stage door of the Civic Center. I asked him what time and he answered "Whenever." I rolled my eyes and thought, *How Deadhead-ish.*

The concert was about an hour away and I didn't want to go alone, so I asked my new friend Val D'Ambrosio to come with me. Val was a young local girl who was the radio station's most devoted worker. She was smart, fun to hang out with, and even though I was more than a couple of years older, we both liked the same music. Val especially loved Tom Petty and I promised her that if she went to the Dead show with me, and drove my car back to Boston, I would make sure she met Tom Petty at his upcoming show at the Orpheum Theatre.

The parking lot at the Civic Center was almost full. There were hundreds of people hanging out and everyone wanted to sell us drugs. I saw a large group of girls standing at the side of the building and I knew it had to be the door where I was supposed to meet Bob Weir. Val and I pushed through the crowd and I yelled my name to the security guard. My name wasn't on any list and I was about to leave. I was also about to sucker punch the skanky bimbo on acid who was leaning into me, screaming in my ear. Just in time, I saw Bob and the band walking by. Somehow our eyes met, and he reached over the crowd, grabbed my hand, and dragged me inside. I turned and waved to Val, tossing her my car keys at the very last second before the door slammed. I looked up at Bob, who was smiling as if he planned the whole thing.

Two minutes later I was onstage with the Grateful Dead. Bob shoved a baggie in my hand as he led me to a chair that was set up on the right side of the stage next to

Mickey Hart's drums. The lights went out and the crowd started screaming and I started rolling. As they began playing "New Minglewood Blues", a crazed Deadhead slid down the aisle on his knees and crashed into the stage headfirst. Security guards took him away on a stretcher. I kept rolling joints and handing them out to the backstage crew whenever the lights dimmed. That happened a lot and I wasn't sure why. The Dead seemed to be tuning up but the Deadheads kept twirling anyway. Finally, an actual song started and it was one of the few that I knew the words to. Looking around at the frenzied crowd, I realized this was no Bruce Springsteen concert. It did however last just as long.

"Deal" closed the first ten-song set. I thought the show was over and as I left the stage I said to Bob, "That was great. I thought it was going to be a lot longer. I liked the part where you seemed like you were tuning up, but that wasn't what you were doing, right?" I babbled on. I could feel the stares of everyone around me but Bob thought it was hilarious and when he started laughing, so did they. I didn't feel as dumb as they looked. The second set started with "Alabama Getaway" and ended nineteen songs later, with "Around and Around". During "drums", Mickey Hart stood up, jumped off the drum kit and walked over to his giant gong just a couple of feet from me and yelled "Pay attention! I get a hard-on during this one." And he did. The encore was "U.S. Blues".

Bob turned to me and delivered the best pick up line I ever heard. "Wanna go back to my room and go through my bag of pills?"

The Deadheads were camped out in the lobby of the hotel when Bob and I pulled up in a white limo. They chased us to the elevator, tried to squeeze in when the doors started to close, and were running down the hallway when we got to Bob's room. Inside, I was pleasantly surprised to see an actual Ziploc baggie filled with a lot of different pills. He handed me one and I gulped it down with a warm glass of funky smelling tap water from the bathroom sink. I was afraid the water would somehow contaminate my body but never gave the pill a second thought. Someone knocked on the door and to my surprise Bob answered it. There stood a Deadhead couple and a dog. The guy held the dog and proudly said it was born at a Dead show and they named it Jerry. Bob said he'd be sure to let Jerry know and politely asked them to leave. They just laughed and sat down across the hall as Bob shut the door. I tried to forget about them and concentrate on Bob who was starting to undress me. He put his arms around me and started kissing my neck as he asked me if he was my first rock 'n' roll tomcat. I smiled but didn't laugh, and I couldn't answer since Bob was sticking his tongue in my ear and down my throat. My knees started to buckle and he kept kissing me as we collapsed on the bed.

Sex with Bob was like a taking a Quaalude mixed with LSD. It seemed to be happening in slow motion complete with those pesky "tracers". Bob and I rolled around on the bed and he ended up on top. He was pressing into me but not too much, just letting me that know he was ready. Sweat from his hair dropped onto my breasts. Then the "sparkling" happened. When the drops landed on me I could see them splashing on my skin in beautiful colors. Bob leaned down and licked the sweat off my breasts and then he collapsed on top of me. After about five minutes of heavy breathing, he rolled me over and we did it again.

I woke up in Bob's arms I couldn't believe how well I had slept. I was refreshed not hung over. I wanted more of those pills, so when Bob got up and went into the bathroom to take a shower I searched the room for the bag of pills but it was nowhere to be found. I didn't have to dig to learn all about Bob. He was happy to tell me about himself though I assumed most of it was made up. Bob's parents, he said, were literally rocket scientists and he ran away and joined this Grateful Dead circus as a rebellious kid of fourteen. He told me he was dyslexic, and he had a dog named Otis. He checked into hotels under the name "Mr. Wonderful". Luckily, he didn't ask anything about me. I wasn't as good as Bob was with sharing stuff, even if it was a lie.

There was a knock at the door and Jerry Garcia walked into the room. I was sitting up in bed and if Jerry saw me he pretended I wasn't there. He and Bob started having a conversation about something and Bob kept trying to change the subject and talk about a problem he had with the next album cover. The Grateful Dead's *Go to Heaven* was going to be released on April 28, 1980 and there was a misprint on the back cover. Bob's song "Feel Like a Stranger" was listed as "*Feels* Like a Stranger" and he wanted it changed. Jerry didn't seem to hear him and left the room while Bob was in the middle of a sentence. I felt like I should say something so I asked Bob how the band decisions were made. He just shook his head and started packing. Bob had two piles of shirts. Blue button downs and black T-shirts. He had dozens of them and he put them in a suitcase with a hair dryer and was all packed.

I got dressed and we tried to leave the hotel. The band had a day off and we were going to eat at some restaurant they all liked. We got in a van and started to drive away with the Deadheads following on foot. Rock Scully was the Grateful Dead's road manager and he looked like Keith Richard's brother. The one who let himself go. Rock stood at the front of the bus scowling. I thought it would be a good idea if Bob told Rock what was bothering him so I urged him to seize the moment. Bob was reluctant but I didn't let it go. I called Rock over and said "Bob has a problem with the album cover, don't you Bob?"

Rock was not amused. "Are you in this band?" he screamed at me. "Are you in this fucking band?"

I was ready to die. "No," I quivered.

"Then shut the fuck up!" Rock yelled at me.

Everyone on the bus was silent. What had I gotten myself

into? That night before I met Val for my ride back to

Boston, I told Bob I would love to see him again, but I had

to stay away from the whole band thing. He pretended he

knew what I was talking about.

9

On March 27, 1980, two days after my twenty-eighth birthday, I got an unexpected gift that kept on giving for years to come. Daryl Hall, the tall blond half of Hall & Oates, was promoting his solo album *Sacred Songs*. He came to WCOZ to record an interview with me. There was a photographer in the studio and as we posed for photos it felt a little awkward. I couldn't tell what Daryl thought of me at first. He was so tall and looked good while I felt so small and ugly with my bad perm.

I was surprised when Daryl hit on me. I honestly

didn't see it coming. Daryl was really beautiful and he was

blonder than anyone I had ever seen, except maybe Daryl

Hannah. He was tall and lean and dressed in black leather

and I figured he was someone who only fucked

supermodels. I felt like I looked like John Oates standing

next to him. The "hit on me moment" came after the

general manager walked into the studio and, thinking we

were alone, he handed me a videotape and said, "Thanks for *Debbie Does Dallas*. What else ya got?" Daryl started to laugh, the G.M. got red in the face, and I stumbled through the mandatory introduction. When we were alone, Daryl stared into my eyes and said, "So, you want to go watch that movie somewhere?"

Boss Number Two was staying at his girlfriend's apartment, and I could go to the condo. We talked a little. We discovered we had Pennsylvania in common. Daryl was from Pottstown and went to Temple University. So we had a connection. I don't know why we went through the boring chitchat. I wasn't interested in Daryl's story and he wasn't into hearing mine. Thankfully we didn't have many of those forced conversations. Daryl wasn't into drugs. He liked Moët & Chandon White Star champagne. I was surprised how much fun it was to roll around the condo's living room floor while Daryl tied my hands together. I looked over at the television as Debbie did Dallas and

Daryl did me. Sex with Daryl was like being on Ecstasy. Even though we'd just met, I felt a euphoric sense of intimacy and it was just dangerous enough to make it memorable. I wanted to immediately do it again.

The next night I was the M.C. of the Squeeze show at the Paradise on Commonwealth Avenue. Daryl said he'd meet me there and we'd sneak out together after the show started. I didn't want anyone to know that we were hooking up. There were several other girl DJs in town, and Daryl didn't want to alienate the very people who were clamoring to spend some time with him. We worked out a plan to meet at my white Toyota Corolla, which was parked in the front of the club. Daryl and I decided to leave about twenty minutes after I introduced the band. As I was screaming into the microphone "Please give a warm WCOZ welcome to Squeeze!" I saw Daryl in the audience surrounded by a bunch of fans and some of the other DJs. He smiled at me and I really wanted to get out there and be with him. How difficult could it be to pull this off?

While darting out of the club minutes later I ran into my boss, who asked me to go to the truck (which was how we used to broadcast live shows on the radio) and hang around until the show ended to read the thank you list and say the goodbyes. The truck was parked right next to my car. I tried to get to Daryl before he got to my car but when people started to gather by the truck, he deftly jumped into my car and hid in the back seat. He thought he'd only be there for a few minutes but the six-foot-one Daryl had to curl up in my car's tiny back seat for at least a half hour.

People were asking for Daryl and I kept saying he was in

the club watching the show so they'd go back inside to look

for him. At any moment he could have been seen hiding in

my car if anyone had looked inside though the window.

When I was finally able to get away, I jumped in the

driver's seat of my car and took off down Commonwealth

Avenue. Daryl and I laughed all the way back to his hotel.

After Daryl left town I realized what less is more

meant. I couldn't wait to see him again, but it was time to

get back to my life. Maybe this was the way to have it all. I

wondered who my next sexcapades partner would be.

Things were now going pretty well in Beantown. So what if

it's cold and I miss Philly? I started to believe I could make

this work.

One night I was on the air playing side 2 of Pink

Floyd's *Dark Side of the Moon* when I got a phone call

from Program Director # 1 from Philly. I didn't think there

was anything he could say that would interest me. That is until he offered me a job at KLOS in Los Angeles. Who in their right mind would turn that down?

My last show on WCOZ was on April 11, 1980. The next day I was on American Airlines Flight 49 to Los Angeles. I couldn't wait to swap my L.L. Bean for Fred Segal.

On April 17 I did my first show on KLOS, the WMMR of Los Angeles. I knew nothing about the station's esteemed history and no one knew who the hell I was. And to make it even more awkward, my first two program directors were now working together. They were the new general manager and program director at KLOS. As the Who song goes: "Meet the new boss, same as the old boss."

I didn't have sufficient time to find an apartment and all my stuff was on a moving van slowly crossing the country. My new bosses let me check into the Valley Hilton on Ventura Blvd in Sherman Oaks and I rented a temporary company car. My car was being driven across the country by a woman I'd never met. She placed an ad in a Boston newspaper and I gave her the keys without a second thought. I wasn't getting any phone call updates from her so I really didn't think I'd ever see her or my car again. The good news was that my friends who directed and produced *The Buddy Holly Story* were back in L.A. making their second movie called *Under The Rainbow*.

I was thrilled to be on the radio again, but just like Boston, I didn't feel the listeners' love like I had in Philadelphia. Dusty Street was a very popular DJ on KLOS. She was the 10 P.M. to 2 A.M. DJ and had just the right personality and attitude for the rock audience in Los Angeles. I wanted to sound more like her but didn't know how to do it. She tried to help me learn the L.A. way of doing rock radio. It was tough for me to fill the shoes of the man I replaced: B. Mitchell Reed. He was the man Joni Mitchell wrote "Rainy Night House" about and he was beloved by the KLOS listeners. Nonetheless, I felt a little better in the sunshine of L.A. than I did in Boston. I loved L.A. and just needed to figure out how to make my new listeners love me.

After three weeks in the hotel I moved into a one-bedroom apartment on 241 S. Doheny Drive in Beverly Hills. It's considered "Beverly Hills adjacent", which meant it was the poor side of the very rich town. The moving van finally brought my belongings and my car even eventually arrived. I settled into my daily radio show and things seemed to be going pretty well. Every day in Los Angeles is another "shitty day in paradise," as I heard J.R. Ewing himself, Larry Hagman, say one day in Malibu. The weather was just as great as it was in Mexico and I was out having fun and hearing music almost every night. In La-La Land, even a bad night was pretty fucking great. The

Sunset Strip was better than advertised. My neighborhood hangouts were now The Roxy Theatre, The Whiskey a Go Go, and the Rainbow Bar & Grill. And all over Hollywood there were clubs like The Starwood, Gazzarri's, and the Troubadour where the best glam rock bands played every night.

And being back in Los Angeles, I thought about Warren all the time. I really wanted to see him again and wondered if he was still married.

On May 16, 1980 KLOS sent listeners to the movie premiere of *The Hollywood Knights*. I was paid a small appearance fee to show up at Mann's Chinese Theatre in Hollywood and greet them. I decided to buy a corset to wear under the tight fitting dress I planned to wear so I drove to Trashy Lingerie on North La Cienega Boulevard. Leaving the store, I got a call from Jeb Brien who worked for Champion Entertainment. He told me Daryl Hall was in town. I said I'd meet up with him after the movie premiere.

I wouldn't even stop to change my clothes since I knew Daryl was going to love the corset.

Daryl's hotel room had a couple of huge mirrors on the wall next to the bed. He turned up the lights and I was out of my dress in about three seconds. I started to unhook the front of the corset but Daryl told me to leave it on. When I looked in the mirror I couldn't believe how we looked. It was like a porno family portrait. I was on my side, wearing nothing but my corset and Daryl was stretched out behind me. He was pushing up against me with his arms around me; his hands grabbing at my breasts. I continued to stare at myself in the mirror. I noticed Daryl was also staring at himself. He was beautiful. His skin was very pale and he had one small black ink tattoo on his upper arm near his shoulder.

One night, while driving on Sunset Boulevard, I heard the Neil Young song "Like a Hurricane" on the radio. It has and always will be the song that most describes my feelings for Warren Zevon. By the time Neil sang the words "I am just a dreamer but you are just a dream," I knew I had to see Warren again. The feelings I had for Warren were a mystery to me. And I had no defense. I took a psychology class in college and learned about the three kinds of love. I think what was happening was that the "Eros" type of love that I first felt for Warren was morphing into that crazy "Agape" love, or something like that. I wish I had paid more attention in that class, but "Who knew?" as my mother always says.

On June 24, 1980 I went to see Warren perform at Universal Amphitheatre. My parents were visiting and I took my mom as my "plus one". After the show we went backstage and I saw Bruce Springsteen standing around so I pointed him out to my mother. Before I could stop her she approached Bruce and, in her best Philly accent, she said, "Hi Bruce, I'm from Philly and you're from Jersey." When I saw the blank look on Bruce's face I felt like I had to do something, so I stepped in and introduced my mom to Bruce. He clearly didn't know who I was but he faked it and mumbled something nice. As he turned to walk away my mother said in her loudest most annoying voice, "Boy, he's a real nothing!" I grabbed her by the hand and got out of there without ever seeing Warren.

I found out that Bruce was in Los Angeles to work on *The River* when Danny Federici called me. He said he was flying in to work with Bruce and asked me to pick him up from the airport. I always had fun with Danny and his wife Amy. I don't remember the actual first time we met, but I think it was in Philly in 1978. I remember the three of us in my apartment at Park Towne Place and I know we went dancing at some disco. In addition to being Bruce's band mate, Danny was Bruce's childhood friend. Like a lot of friends who are like brothers, theirs was a complex relationship. Danny was laid-back, loose, and fun, while Bruce was very serious and had a hard time enjoying himself offstage. Danny said he hadn't been in touch with Bruce for a while so he didn't expect Bruce to pick him up at the airport. But when I arrived at the gate there Bruce was. In 1980 in Los Angeles, Bruce Springsteen could still walk around all by himself, headband and all, without being bothered. Danny got off the plane and saw both of us and didn't know what to do. The three of us stood there awkwardly until finally Danny said to Bruce, "I didn't know you would be here, so I asked Anita to pick me up."

"Oh wow, sure," Bruce stammered. "Whatever you want to do. I'll just meet you at the studio on Holloway. You know, the one near the Sunset Marquis." Bruce turned around and was gone in a flash.

Danny and I walked to the parking lot and got into my car. I didn't know what was going on between the two of them but it felt really tense. We arrived at the studio and went inside. Bruce stopped recording and said I had to leave because I was a DJ and they couldn't be trusted. Then he burst into a high-pitched laugh that startled me.

"No problem, I'll go," I said.

Bruce kept talking, "I know you're Danny's friend, but you're on the radio so—"

"I got it, I'm leaving," I said, cutting him off. Ever the gentleman, Bruce insisted on walking me out to my car. Danny came along and as I drove out of the parking lot I saw Bruce put his arm around Danny and walk back inside the studio. It was a sweet moment but such drama! The next day I went to the Sunset Marquis to see Danny. His wife Amy was back in Jersey so we made a sign reading "HELLO AMY" and took a photo of us with it in the mirror. We were laughing loudly when Bruce walked into the room. The three of us went out onto the balcony overlooking the pool. The Sunset Marquis's pool was always a rockin' scene. All the bands staying at the hotel liked to get high and gather there all day. Record promoters would come there to try to do some business but it was too much of a party. I was standing on the balcony with Danny and Bruce when I noticed a man wearing a shiny jacket carrying a rolled up copy of *Billboard* magazine in one hand and a briefcase with backstage passes stuck to it in the other.

"Gee," I said sarcastically, "what business do you think he's in?"

Danny chuckled but Bruce got hysterical and laughed too loudly and way too long. I raised my eyebrows and looked at Danny and we both tried not to laugh.

On July 28 Daryl Hall was in town for a concert at the Greek Theatre. He was staying at the Beverly Hills Hotel. It was a blast hanging out poolside in a cabana eating a Cobb salad. Of course I wasn't paying for anything. Tommy Motolla was footing this bill. Daryl's management company, Champion Entertainment, was founded by Tommy Motolla and he had the staff of the hotel running around trying to do everything to please his client.

One afternoon Daryl introduced me to an actor from New Jersey named Joe. I was immediately attracted to him and he jumped all over me the minute we were alone in the cabana. We had sex while his clueless girlfriend was swimming in the pool. Daryl acted as our lookout, and I could tell he was amused and impressed by my moxie. I felt like a bad girl and it felt really good.

Occasionally Joe would show up at my apartment building and scream my name like Stanley Kowalski until I answered the door. It was usually in the wee hours of the morning and I wanted to get mad but the sex was so good that I just couldn't. I also felt like I had leveled the playing field with Daryl, who always had lots of women around. I was surprised at how good I felt about the fact that there was no jealousy, because neither of us cared enough. I did love Daryl's creative antics until the day he handcuffed me to the towel rack in the bathroom of his hotel room. He had to leave for his show and couldn't find the handcuff's key. I had to hang out, so to speak, naked for about an hour until one of the lucky guys who worked for Champion Entertainment arrived. He had a shit-eating grin on his face and, thankfully, the missing key to the cuffs.

"Say one word and I swear I'll get Daryl to fire you" I tried to say with a straight face.

"Yeah, like that's gonna happen," he laughed as he unlocked the cuffs.

I stood up. My knees hurt from kneeling on the tile floor and they were already turning black and blue. I looked in the mirror and thought I looked so tired. Then I thought of "Lili Von Shtupp" singing "I'm Tired" from the movie *Blazing Saddles* and I burst out laughing. I got dressed and out of there.

On August 15 Warren Zevon played the first of five nights at the Roxy on Sunset Boulevard. He was recording the shows for his live album *Stand in the Fire*. It had been four months since I moved to L.A. and we still hadn't seen each other. I thought this was my chance and I had to go. I also needed to be able to get backstage. Irving Azoff was Warren's manager at that time and we knew each other from Boston when the Eagles, another Irving managed band, came to town, I called and asked him to take me to one of the Roxy shows.

I met Irving at the venue's "will call" window. When we walked in, Irving and I were ushered to a special table to the left of the stage. I looked up and saw the "girlfriend box" where the girlfriends of Neil Young, Jackson Browne, and the Eagles' sat. Probably not Yoko Ono, but maybe May Pang. All of Warren's friends were sitting around me and I started to panic at the thought of seeing Warren again. I swallowed a Quaalude, hoping everything would be okay. When I took them in Mexico, they helped me get through tough situations. But now, in the coked-up eighties, not so much.

After the show, I stumbled backstage on Irving's arm. The room was spinning and the first face I focused on was Warren's. He was wearing a light blue T-shirt that read "KNOTS LANDING". Kim Lankford, one of the stars of that television show, was hanging on his arm. Warren looked at us and winced. Kim led him to the other side of the room. I wanted to call out to him and explain why I was there with

Irving. I wanted to talk to him. Instead I stood there and drooled. I couldn't speak and I could barely stand. The next day when I finally woke up, I realized that Quaaludes were no longer my friend nor part of my life. And neither was Warren. I started to wonder why I came to Los Angeles. I questioned every decision I had made.

I couldn't wait to see Danny and Amy Federici again when Bruce and the Band arrived in October for four shows at the L.A. Sports Arena. There's nothing like a Bruce show to make me feel like I am back in Philly, on my way to the Jersey Shore for the weekend. Danny Federici and I used to joke about being in "Bruce Prison" but in this case I was happy to be an inmate. The night before they arrived I had a sex dream starring Bruce Springsteen. After four hours of sweaty sex, I told him I liked him better when he was younger and he told me I talked too much. Then I woke up.

I got fired from KLOS on September 5, 1980 by my last two program directors. I couldn't believe they had teamed up and were getting back at me for quitting my last two jobs. They claimed it wasn't personal as they broke the news to me over a lunch meeting. I was in shock and too numb to be angry. As I drove home from that awful lunch, I thought about the last year and a half. I had moved from Philadelphia to Boston to Los Angeles and worked for four different radio stations. I was exhausted and my career was a disaster. I went back to my apartment and crawled into bed. I don't cry often but I was sobbing that night. I felt like a fraud and was sure that my success in Philly must have been a fluke. If I hadn't had a friend like Bobbi Silver, I wouldn't have ever been on the radio. I was dreading the reaction of my parents. They had been so supportive and I was such an idiot.

10

My unemployment payments were running out and I had no job prospects. Once again I found solace at a Bruce Springsteen concert. On October 29 I met Amy and Danny Federici at the Sunset Marquis. As usual there was a huge party going on by the pool. I drank too much and I was loopy by the time they left for sound check. As I walked to my car, I saw Clarence Clemons still in a hot tub with a drink in his hand flanked by two beautiful blondes. He smiled and waved at me as I stumbled by. I clipped on my backstage pass and drove to the Sports Arena. I needed a big shot of Bruce, and I got it. The band played thirty-one songs that night.

On Halloween Bruce was carried onto the stage in a coffin. I was sitting alone beside four or five empty seats.

Bruce didn't give the friends and family members the best seats. Those were for the fans. The F.O.B.'s (Friends and Family of the Band) always sat on the side of the venue about midway back. Halfway through the first set, I had to go backstage and find a way to get happier. I walked down the bleachers and made my way to the stage. After showing my pass to the security guy, he waved me through. I walked into an empty dressing room and poured myself a big drink of Remy Martin. Oh yeah, V.S.O.P. that's me. I used the private restroom, stopped for another shot, and made my way back to my seat. At first I thought I had the wrong row because almost all the seats, mine included, were now full. I double-checked the row number and decided to sit in the only empty seat until the intermission.

Once the lights came up I turned to my left to see who was next to me.

It was Bob Dylan.

The first thought I had was, *Someone dosed the Remy Martin.* Then I thought I was having a Bob mirage, but it was really him. *Bob Dylan* was next to me. I wondered if he could hear my heart beating. There were three other people in the row—two women and a man, who I would later find out was drummer Jim Keltner. Max Weinberg gave him the tickets and since he and Bob were recording some new songs at Rundown Studios in Santa Monica, Jim, Bob, and two backup singers came to the show. Bob was talking and I couldn't be sure but it seemed like he was talking to me.

"Is the show over?" Bob said.

"No, it's intermission," I croaked. I looked right into Bob Dylan's eyes but he was focused on my right thigh. My backstage pass that had caught his attention.

"Can I get one of those?" Dylan asked me. I laughed but he was serious.

"You probably don't need a pass to go backstage," I assured him. Bob just looked at me so I continued. "Because you're *Bob Dylan*."

Jim Keltner leaned forward and said, "Yeah, but he doesn't get that."

The second half of the show started and I watched Bob watch Bruce. He didn't seem too into it unless Bruce was playing harmonica. Then he uncrossed his arms and leaned toward the stage. When the show ended and the lights came on Bob said to me "Will you take me backstage?"

I almost fainted but somehow I said, "Let's go." I started to walk down the aisle but decided to let Bob lead. Then I got protective when people started to recognize him so I got back in front of him. He was walking too slowly so I turned around and let him get in front of me but he didn't seem to know which way to go so I took the lead as BOB

DYLAN TOOK MY HAND. We approached the final security guard who smiled and patted Bob on the back as we walked by. I saw Bob grimace as he surveyed the backstage area complete with a sushi chef and lots of mirrors. Everyone backstage was staring at us. A couple of brave people asked Bob to take a photo. He didn't seem to mind when a girl with a Jersey accent asked me to take their picture. I was thrilled when he also posed with me as Jersey Girl clicked away. She promised to give me her phone number but didn't and I never saw those photos. (You know who you are and if you're reading this, I wish you would contact me.) I led Bob over to Bruce's dressing room and announced proudly to the giant sized security guard, "Bob Dylan to see Bruce."

"Give me twenty-five, thirty minutes, please," he answered robotically.

"No, really, Bob Dylan is right here, and he wants to see Bruce," I said with a laugh.

"No really, give me twenty-five minutes," he said with a fake smile.

I turned to Bob and said "Ten or fifteen minutes." As we stood together I saw Bob looking at Robin Williams who was talking to Pam Dawber. "Wow," I joked, "Mork and Mindy." Bob just stared blankly at me. Next I spotted Penny Marshall and Cindy Williams and again I tried a little humor. "Look, Laverne and Shirley!"

Bob cocked his head and said, "The Andrew Sisters?"

I laughed but I knew he wasn't kidding. Then it dawned on me. I was wasting a once in a lifetime moment with Bob Dylan. I took a deep breath and I laid my whole story on him. I told him about my radio jobs and how I got fired and how confused I was and didn't know what to do next, and he seemed to be listening. When I stopped talking I shrugged my shoulders and smiled.

Bob didn't miss a beat.

"Go back to Philly," he said loud and clear.

"What?" I asked him just to be sure.

"Go back to Philly," he repeated and nodded his head as if it was decided.

Just then, the beefy bodyguard in front of Bruce's dressing room waved to me.

"Bruce will see Bob now," he announced.

I nudged Bob to get his attention, pointed toward the bodyguard, and as he started walking away I yelled "Bye, Bob. And thank you."

He gave me an over the head wave and never looked back.

I ran to my car and drove home. It was very clear to me what I needed to do. I called Bobbi Silver and told her

Bob Dylan told me to go back to Philly. She laughed and told me there was a new very cool program director at WMMR that she would call on my behalf.

The next day Charlie Kendall, the new program director, called me.

"Get back here and I'll give you any shift you want," Charlie yelled over a speakerphone.

"But how can you do that?" I shrieked.

"Don't worry about it," he laughed. "Just get back here."

What do you know, I thought, as I started to pack my well-travelled belongings, *Bob was right*. Maybe I hadn't burned every bridge in the Tri-State area, and just maybe I *could* go home again. I wasn't sure what my life would be like but I really believed it would not include Los Angeles.

Nor Warren Zevon.

Thanksgiving came three days early for me that year. I flew back to Philly on November 24, 1980. Charlie at WMMR was a fun, wild, guy. He usually wore a white three-piece suit and ran around the station with a big smile on his face. He didn't care what you were on, as long as you shared it with him. He was out most nights and never acted like he was in charge. I was ecstatic to be back even though I had to move into my parent's condo right outside of Philly until I found an apartment.

I took Charlie at his word that I would be part of the full-time air staff again and soon rented a small one-bedroom in a newly converted building called "Le Chateau" on Rittenhouse Square right across the park from WMMR. I knew that someone would have to lose his job so I could get mine back and I felt a little bit bad about that. But hey, that's radio. Charlie had no problem giving me shifts on the air since it was the week of Thanksgiving and a couple of the DJs were away. I worried that the listeners wouldn't be as happy as I was for me to be back on the air.

I was amazed by the response. The phones lines lit up and as I listened to the incredibly nice things callers said, I thought about Bob Dylan. I felt like the girl in his song "She Belongs to Me". As a narcissist with self-esteem issues it felt really good.

A few afternoons later, Earle Baily was on the air and decided to play Steppenwolf's version of Hoyt Axton's "The Pusher". Big mistake. The song was only allowable at night. Charlie demoted Earle to part-time and that's how I became the not so new midday DJ on WMMR. (Sorry, Earle.)

On December 9, 1980 I was sitting in my parent's TV room watching *Monday Night Football* with my dad. Howard Cosell announced that John Lennon had been shot. The next day I drove to the radio station in a daze, listening to John Lennon sing "Imagine" on WMMR. I didn't know how I was going to do it but I needed to be on the air again. The listeners I spoke to on the request lines helped me make it through my shift by thanking me and the station for being there for them. The murder of John Lennon threatened all my beliefs in peace, love and understanding. I wasn't old enough to fully process the Kennedy Assassination when it happened. John Lennon's senseless death is something I don't think I will ever come to terms with. I'm sure anyone who remembers that day had no idea how much things would change in the world.

The word "stalker" replaced the word "streaker" in the headlines and no one was laughing anymore. It even trickled down to the concert-going experience which, sadly, would never be the same. Security concerns became the most important thing and who could blame the bands? Since the disastrous 1969 Rolling Stones Altamont Concert or the Who's deadly 1979 Cincinnati show, I understand why the security measures needed to be stronger. But after John Lennon's death, it seemed like the security measures went too far in the other direction. If Courtney Cox went to a Bruce Springsteen concert in real life, that spontaneously shared dance would have never happened. When she rushed the stage, security guards would have beat the shit out of her.

I saw most of the concerts in Philly at a bunch of great venues. From small clubs like Bijou, Mann Music Center, The Tower, The Academy of Music, and, of course, the Spectrum. Barbara Rose was one of the few women in the business. As the assistant to concert promoter Larry Magid for Electric Factory Concerts, Barbara worked every show. One of her many thankless tasks included deciding who got the backstage passes and the press box tickets. I spent many nights backstage before, during, and after shows, and it was a thrill for me every time. There was food and liquor and I got to see the bands arrive in their limos in the underground tunnel. Sometimes I would follow the band to the stage and once in a while, depending on who was performing, I could walk up the steps and onto the stage. The spotlights blinded me and I would always stumble over a microphone cord on the floor. When the audience started to scream and the band plugged in their guitars it was the most exciting thing I ever felt. I was terrified when I had to get on the stage at the Spectrum and introduce a band. Someone had to push me out there but then someone had to yell at me and tell me get *off* the stage. After only a couple of minutes in front of the fans, I had to sit down and drink a shot of something. I understood the lure of the live show and the power of the live audience.

The first time I met Nils Lofgren it was January 21, 1981. He was on tour to support his solo album, *Night Fades Away*. I went to his show at Starr's, a small club on Philly's famous South Street which later became Ripley's Music

Hall. Nils played guitar like Jimi Hendrix and he performed insane gymnastic moves. He left the stage for a couple of minutes during a long guitar solo and from where I stood against the wall I could see Nils just offstage peeing into a trash can. He never stopped playing and I was intrigued. Nils had been playing and recording music since he was seventeen. When he was eighteen he joined Neil Young's band and played piano and guitar and sang on *After the Gold Rush*. In 1972 Nils joined the band Crazy Horse, and in 1973 he played on Neil Young's *Tonight's the Night*.

I went upstairs to his dressing room after the show and we started to talk and ended up going out to Dobb's at 304 South Street. I loved the dump. It was dark and had a tiny stage and a disgusting bathroom. We slid into a booth and started to make out like junior high school kids. His hands are really big and he was moving them all over my body. My skin felt hot and I was sticking to the vinyl booth. Nils was just about my size so our bodies fit well together. Sex with Nils was like smoking really good hashish. More like black hash, earthy and organic. As a gymnast (a big plus), he's very limber. Nils was gentle but forceful as he pushed himself into me. He did it all and all I had to do was enjoy it.

Unlike most musicians I've known, even after a grueling concert, Nils wanted to play some more. He loved to play live, anywhere, with just about anyone. After a couple of brews Nils would jump onstage anywhere and ask, "Do you guys know, 'Stand by Me'?" Just like that,

Nils instantly melded with musicians he'd never met let alone played with. Although there was no real love connection between us, I liked being around Nils. We spent a lot of time together in the studio when Nils recorded his album *Flip* at the Warehouse. Nils booked studio time in the afternoon and the guys from Bon Jovi were recording their second album, *7800° Fahrenheit*, at night. Nils liked to have dinner at the same sushi restaurant, Hikaru on 607 South 2nd Street, almost every night. I remember how he always ordered and ate dessert first. Nils was so easy to be around. There was no spoiled rock star behavior. No tantrums or mood swings. Nils was all about music, sushi, and sex. When he couldn't sleep Nils would sit up all night filing his finger picks into the perfect shape. Nils had been on stages all around the world playing with Neil Young but didn't try to be worldly. The morning after we met for the first time, I ordered poached eggs for breakfast. After the waiter took our order, Nils told me he was glad I ordered them that way since he'd always wanted to see what they were.

I was happier than ever being back in Philly, and once again being part of WMMR. I was even getting better at the interview thing.

On February 1, 1981 I was featured in an article by Matt Damsker for the *Philadelphia Bulletin*. I had left the Focus/Food section of the newspaper behind and was now in the Entertainment section. The headline was ANITA'S MORE THAN JUST A PRETTY VOICE.

> When Anita Gevinson said
>
> goodbye to Philadelphia a
>
> couple of years ago, she
>
> at least had the
>
> satisfaction of knowing
>
> she'd set the town's radio
>
> community on fire. After

two short-lived stints in Boston and Los Angeles, WMMR program director Charlie Kendall wasted little time in putting Anita back on the air. The twenty-eight-year-old Levittown native is back where she and her listeners figure she belongs, on WMMR rocking from 10 A.M. to 2 P.M. each weekday. "You've got to realize that I didn't want to leave Philadelphia in the first place," explained Anita, an engaging woman whose radio style blends salty

good humor with an

obvious enthusiasm for

rock 'n roll. Her natural,

free-swinging style owes

refreshingly little to the

clichéd, sultry-voiced,

come-hither mold that

once prevailed among

female deejays on the FM

band.

Matt Damsker described me as "cheerfully single".

On March 19, 1982 Warren was on the cover of *Rolling Stone.* In the article titled THE CRACK UP AND RESURRECTION OF WARREN ZEVON, he talked about how he saved himself from "a coward's death" by going to rehab.

He also talked about his wife and how much she helped him get through it. I felt strangely saddened by Warren's good news.

In April, Hall & Oates were on their Spring Fling tour. They had a show at Penn State University so Daryl and I got to have another little fling. After the show we got into a car driven by the handcuff key guy. We dropped him off at his hotel and Daryl slid behind the wheel. We drove to a XXX (as we used to call them) movie theatre on Market Street. The streets were snowy and we were freezing so after parking the car Daryl and I ran into the theatre. When we decided to leave and rush home to have sex at my apartment, neither of us could remember what kind of car we came in or where it was parked. After trying to unlock every car on the block we eventually found ours and drove back to Rittenhouse Square.

Luckily, we still had enough porn fueled feelings to be able to get back to my tiny one bedroom apartment in Le

Chateau at 19th and Walnut Streets. I had barely opened the door when Daryl pushed me onto the floor and ducked into my kitchen to grab a carving knife. He kept his raincoat on while he tied me up and with the knife in one hand he slid his other hand between my legs. I couldn't believe how turned on I was. Daryl put the knife down and pulled my pants off then he picked up the knife and cut off my underpants. He was on top of me on the living room rug as my hands were tied together over my head. I should have been scared or at least uncomfortable but I had an award-winning orgasm. Orgasms can be as tricky as origami, but not that night.

The next morning Daryl was hungry so I made scrambled eggs before taking a quick shower. When I returned to the kitchen all the eggs were gone and Daryl said, "Aren't you going to have anything to eat?" I liked that he could be so regular and such a freak at the same time. This was so much more fun and much easier than having a "real" relationship. I didn't have to talk about anything I was or wasn't feeling. Daryl almost never talked about his personal life since everyone knew about "Sara Smile". He did tell me that whenever he's at home he wants to be on the road, and whenever he's on the road, he wants to be at home. I thought that was sad, but I would soon understand what he meant. Relationships on the road keep moving and when you're trying to have the same thing at home, it's very tough. As Woody Allen says in *Annie Hall*, "A relationship, I think, is like a shark, you know? It has to constantly move forward or it dies."

11

April marked WMMR's thirteenth anniversary and I felt lucky to be celebrating with my fellow DJs Michael Picozzi, Joe Bonnadonna, John Stevens, Tom Robinson, Earle Bailey, and Michael Tearson. My relationship with my listeners was going very well. WMMR was *the* station to listen to and I was enjoying my popularity. My job was like a pot party with great music. Some of the DJs liked to chop and snort but not me. Only pot for me.

Program director Charlie Kendall thought it would be a good idea to not tell me who was scheduled to stop by the radio station for a live on air chat. He felt I was better when I was caught off guard and had to wing it. I thought he was crazy but Charlie insisted. At any moment the studio door would open and I was suddenly interviewing Steve Winwood, or a couple of the guys in Van Halen, the

Pretenders, or Aerosmith's Joe Perry. (For a moment I thought it was Steve Perry, whoops.) Most of the time Charlie was right. I was the only girl on the air staff and I used that to my advantage at times. Everyone I interviewed had so much fun that sometimes they stayed so long they didn't have time to go to the other radio stations. That gave WMMR an exclusive interview and caused a lot of trouble in the Philly radio and record world

Steve Winwood's "people" warned me about his shyness and told me to "go easy on him". Obviously, I have a problem with authority. By the way, Steve isn't really that shy.

Daryl Hall and John Oates were frequent guests on my show even though I once described them as being "much more than 2 stools on stage". Bobbi Silver brought them to the station along with their manager, Champion Entertainment's Jeb Brien. They sat down for a "photo op" with me and Bobbi and WMMR's staff members Lisa Richards, Steve Lushbaugh,, John Bloodwell, and Charlie Kendall.

Another day at the office with Chubby Checker

The only things I remember about the time I spent with Van Halen's Alex Van Halen and Michael Anthony are a lot of laughs and a lot of stripes!

WMMR's Michael Tearson, the "record guy"; Michael Lessner; me; special guest, Fee Waybill of the "Tubes"; Tom Robinson; Joe Bonadonna; and Steve Lushbaugh.

There was one embarrassing moment. A tall handsome man in an overcoat walked into the studio. I had no idea who he was so I kept playing music to buy some time. I was hoping someone else would enter the studio and force an introduction. It didn't happen. At first my mystery guest seemed to enjoy watching and listening to me, but I could tell he was losing patience. He finally figured out my

dilemma and said, "You have no idea who I am, do you?"

"No," I admitted quietly

"I'm Nick Mason," he declared

"I need more," I said sheepishly

He was shocked but amused. "I'm the drummer for

Pink Floyd."

"*Now* we can do the interview," I said proudly.

My "fan mail" was pouring in. I rarely had time to read it

all but one package caught my attention. Someone had sent

me rubber gloves. Not the type used to clean the house, the

medical variety. I was sort of creeped out. On Mother's

Day, my mom, who I nicknamed "Happenin' Janet" was a

special guest on my show. The other guest was Roger

Glover, the bass player for Deep Purple. He was on a

promotional tour for his solo project with a band called Rainbow. Roger was funny and flirty and I loved his English accent and the way he seemed to enjoy meeting my mother. He admitted he was the one who sent the rubber gloves and explained it was a promotional item for the album called *Difficult to Cure*. The album cover featured doctors wearing rubber gloves. Roger left with my phone number and he called a couple of days later to invited me to visit him at his home in Greenwich, Connecticut.

My friend Jessica Velmans lived in New York so I took the Amtrak Metroliner train into the city and headed for her Soho loft on Prince Street. I'd met Jessica when she was producing a local Philly TV show called *People Are Talking*, hosted by Maury Povich. We became fast friends and continued to hang out after she got a job as a producer at ABC in New York.

Roger Glover drove into the city from Connecticut and met Jessica and I for lunch. Roger seemed relieved that neither Jessica nor I were acting like Deep Purple fans. Because we weren't. We had a great time and laughed a lot and Roger definitely got the seal of approval from Jessica. A leisurely lunch and a bottle of wine later, Roger and I jumped into his Jeep and hit the road.

Roger lived in a mansion and it was spectacular. Tennis great Ivan Lendl lived a couple of acres away. After more wine from his very large collection, Roger cooked dinner for the two of us in his very large kitchen, while wearing an album cover on his head.

After dinner we rolled around naked on the floor of his gigantic living room and I found out that *everything* about Roger was large. Okay, I'll say it. Bigger *is* better. Sex with Roger was like being on two lines of crystal meth with a wine back. A really expensive red wine. Roger didn't need to do anything out of the ordinary. Every position was enhanced, if I may make the pun, by his voluminous endowment. It felt like I was participating in the Olympics of sex. I was the tough Russian judge who still gave Roger lots of 10's.

The next day he prepared breakfast and we watched a movie on TV starring Martin Mull called *Serial*. Then we started drinking the delicious red wine again. I don't remember much about the movie, but I do recall that I was wearing only a pair of grey and white striped tights. Roger asked me to pose for him and he sketched a picture of me from behind. He put down the pencil and we fell on the floor. Roger was ready to go again and I was just trying to keep up. We fell asleep and when I came to, all I could think was: *What the hell was in that wine? Who eats baked beans for breakfast? Could we have sex again, please?*

The weekend came to an end and I had to go back to Philly. Jessica, who was at her parent's house in Sheffield, Massachusetts, drove to Greenwich and picked me up. Roger walked me out to her car and I distinctly caught Jessica staring directly at the bulge in his tight leather pants. We drove off and I said to Jessica, "It was fun, but not a love connection."

"Maybe you could learn to love him," Jessica said, as we both laughed.

I wondered if I ever would find a true love. I didn't think so, but it was sure fun trying.

In July, Stevie Nicks was promoting her *Bella Donna* album which I couldn't stop playing. The songs spoke to me and the vocals and melodies stayed in my head for weeks. I did something I never did. I tried to schedule an interview with Stevie. Paul Fishkin, the co-founder of Modern Records, was easy to get on the telephone but pinning him down about the interview wasn't as easy. He said something like "I'll see what I can do." Whatever he did to get Stevie to come to WMMR in the middle of the day worked.

I was waiting around after my shift, trying not to be too disappointed, when Stevie Nicks walked in. I gulped, took a deep breath and escorted her into a small studio to record our interview. I was more nervous than usual because I didn't think I could play the flirting game like I usually did. But I did it anyway. The more I gushed, the more Stevie talked, and she really loosened up. I thought she might be telling some of the stories for the first time, but probably not. She revealed that she wrote "Leather and Lace" for Waylon Jennings and Jessi Colter to record and explained how she ended up singing it with Don Henley.

Stevie was even up for recording promos for the radio station and gamely repeated "Hi, I'm Stevie Nicks and when I'm in Philadelphia I listen to 93.3 WMMR" about half a dozen times. When I left the room for a couple of minutes, Stevie signed the cover of my album: "To Anita, for loving the songs. Stevie". I beamed for a week.

After the interview, Stevie was happy to pose with WMMR's John Stevens, Tom Robinson and Charlie

Kendall.

On September 24, 1981 the Rolling Stones came to Philly for two nights at JFK Stadium They were landing at the Philadelphia International Airport at a private landing strip. I found out about it from John Bloodwell, the biggest Rolling Stones fan I have ever met. John worked at WMMR and was responsible for creating the "A to Z" specials. He came up with the idea of playing all the songs of the Rolling Stones in alphabetical order. The ratings were great and soon many stations all over the country were using the A to Z concept. John and I became friends over our mutual love of Mick and Keith. When John came into the studio and told me he was going to the airport to meet the Stones' plane and asked if I wanted to come along, I asked no questions. We drove in John's big old sedan. I knew John had this. Sure enough, we pulled into a small area with a guard booth and John handed the guy a business card. "We're here to meet the Rolling Stones," John said to the confused rent a cop. "Please make sure no one else gets in."

"Okay, sure" was all the guard could say.

We pulled in and there were three black vans waiting with engines running. When I saw the small plane landing I got out of the car. I was wearing a WMMR baseball cap and held it tightly so it wouldn't fly away. The plane stopped and the steps came down and there they were. Mick started walking toward us and John stuck out his hand and Mick reached out and shook it. I don't know how I thought of it but I took the baseball cap off of my head and handed it to Mick. He said something but I was too crazed to really hear it and then he turned and followed the others into the vans. John and I ran back to his car and followed the band all the way to JFK. Unfortunately the guard at the stadium wasn't so easily fooled by John's business card routine and we were turned away. Still, it was a great moment and we laughed all the way home while we smoked a fat one. The next morning on the cover of the *Philadelphia Daily News* was a picture of Mick Jagger wearing my WMMR baseball cap. I went to the station and told the story and everyone went crazy.

The Grateful Dead had a show at Stabler Arena in Bethlehem, Pennsylvania the next day, so Bob Weir and Mickey Hart were also in Philly. They stopped by WMMR to co-host my show and had a blast reading the weather and talking about the music we played. Mickey Hart is a natural comic and Bob had a hard time keeping up. Bob looked cuter than ever and I was happy to see him. Mickey noticed our mutual attraction and said to me, "Baby, you and me are showbiz; you and Bob are just puppy love." I went to the Dead show instead of the Stones' that night, so I was thrilled when Bob said he was going to the Stones' the next night and invited me to come along.

On June 17, 1978 the Stones performed before one hundred thousand fans at JFK but it got rowdy and the audience trashed the stage, causing about a million dollars in damage. But here they were coming back to Philly with legendary concert promoter Bill Graham. When the Rolling Stones started to make their way to the stage, Bill Graham screamed at the top of his lungs, "Everybody step back and no eye contact with the band!" He looked like he would kill you if you didn't listen to him. The show was incredible and this time the fans behaved. The doors opened at 11 A.M. with George Thorogood and the Delaware Destroyers—and destroy they did. Mick Jagger donned a Philadelphia Eagles jersey and we danced all night.

The Jefferson Airplane's Marty Balin walked into the WMMR studio the afternoon of his show at Starr's on South Street. If you've seen the Rolling Stones' Altamont concert film you'll remember that Marty took the punch from a Hell's Angel. He had just released a solo album called *Balin* and halfway through the interview I was more than a little turned on. There was something going on with him besides the obvious major rock star cred. That night I went to the show and at first I thought I was imagining it but a friend who was standing next to me saw it too. Marty Balin was singing *to me*. After the show we went backstage and Marty invited me to dinner. We sat with about fifteen people at a long, loud table and Marty started to talk about his upcoming trip to New York. He asked me to meet him at the Plaza Hotel that weekend and I was about to pretend I had to think about it when I heard someone crying. I looked up and saw a girl trying to get to our table but she was being held back by one of Marty's guys. She called out

Marty's name as they dragged her away. Marty, along with everyone at the table, looked over for a nanosecond before getting on with the meal. *Stalker*, I thought to myself. Marty just smiled at me and repeated his New York offer and I said yes. He walked me out to the street, hailed a taxi, and before I got in Marty grabbed and kissed me hard. I fell asleep that night thinking about when I was fifteen and bought Jefferson Airplane's *Surrealistic Pillow* at the Two Guys department store in Levittown.

I couldn't wait to meet him at the Plaza Hotel. When I walked into its lobby, I held my breath until Marty answered the house phone. We soon got naked and jumped into the bed. I stretched out on the really nice sheets. Marty flipped me over on my stomach and I put my hands against the headboard. We rocked the bed until it started to hit the wall and make too much noise. I needed a quick time-out. Marty looked me over as I tried to catch my breath and told me I was pretty. I was surprised by how romantic he was.

He grabbed a couple of pillows and put them underneath me before getting back on top. I couldn't believe I'd never thought of doing that before. I was drenched in sweat and very grateful to be in a beautiful hotel room in New York with a rock star.

I woke up to Marty singing in the shower. As I'd soon discover, Marty sang all the time. He'd break into song in taxicabs, at restaurants to the delight of the waitress, and while walking in the West Village. It was a crisp fall day and I felt like I was starring in my own Woody Allen movie. I decided to stop wondering about Marty's real life and just enjoy New York. Marty and I strolled hand in hand around Greenwich Village as he pointed out a favorite bookstore of Jim Morrison's or a bar that was a regular haunt of Grace Slick's. I could see our reflection in the store windows and I thought we looked like we'd known each other for a long time instead of it being our first date. That afternoon we went to the movies and saw Neil Simon's *Only When I Laugh* starring Marsha Mason and Kristy McNichol. I kept turning to my right to see Marty staring at me instead of the movie and I was beyond flattered. Walking back to the Plaza, I told him about my day at the Atlantic City Pop Festival and how my dad wouldn't let me stay overnight. He said I must have a great dad. Good answer.

Marty had a show at The Savoy Theatre the night of October 6. We woke up that morning and turned on the TV to find news of the assassination of Egypt's president, Anwar Sadat. Marty turned to me and said, "Sadat's dat." He's charming *and* funny.

The following night we attended *Rolling Stone* magazine's anniversary bash on a rooftop overlooking Central Park. I looked around the room and took it all in. It was hard to believe I was at a party with Marianne Faithful and Roy Orbison and my date was Marty Balin.

I hated to leave Marty and New York but I had that radio job.

Marty called one night and told me he was going on tour and asked for my address. A couple of days later I got a card in the mail from him. It had a naked couple on the front, embracing in some sort of enchanted garden. Inside, Marty wrote that he had no plans to come east, and how it's too bad, since a tumble with me would be worth it. Then he wrote "Keep in touch" and signed it "Love, Marty Balin." A couple of weeks later, the postcards started to arrive. The ones he sent from Cannes and Tokyo were harmless enough. Marty wrote about his tour and the sights he saw. But the one from Mt. Fuji included the name and phone number of his upcoming hotel in Paris. He told me to call him there or drop him a line and signed it "Thinking of you. Love, Marty Balin." A postcard from Portugal had a huge cannon on the front. Marty wrote that he was reading *The White Hotel*, and when he fell asleep he had a dream about me. Then he added, "And you know what we were doing in it, I'm sure." This one was signed "Marty"—no last name.

I was flattered by all the attention but had a problem believing Marty was unattached.

I was right because he had a girlfriend. At least one. And boy was she mad when she opened the love letter I sent him.

Earlier, when we were in New York together, Marty told me to pick a place that the two of us could go on a vacation to some time. I didn't think he was serious, but after all the postcards I started to believe it could happen. I sent him a funny but sexy letter along with a brochure for a resort called La Samanna in St. Bart's. I was ready to leave for work one morning when my phone rang and I almost let it go. Instead I cheerily answered cheerily, "Hello, it's Anita. How can I help you?"

The girl on the other end started screaming at me. "You're not going anywhere with Marty Balin!"

"Who is this?" I asked.

"My name is Barbara!" she screamed.

She hung up before I could ask, "Like Streisand?'

On December 14,1981, an article by Rosemary Parrillo ran in the *Courier Post*. It was called PHILLY'S ON-THE-AIR-WOMEN, featuring me described as "wild and punky" and WIOQ's Helen Leicht as "mellow and smooth":

Helen is a bottle of

Almaden wine by the

fireplace with a mellow

James Taylor tune playing

on the stereo. She'd gaze

into your eyes and tell you

how beautiful they are.

Anita is a bottle of

Catawba Pink and two

tickets to a Clash concert.

She has the hard-hitting

style of a carnival barker,

she gets your attention

and then dares you to step

right up and take your

chances. "People who call

in want abuse. It's like Don Rickles. They want to be known as someone 'Anita' dumped on," she boasts. She packs a lot of fun and entertainment into her four hours on the air. Anita is the brainchild of the 'All Nude Noon News' which starts whenever Anita and her news partner Lorraine Ballard get around to it. "I'm actually not as obnoxious as I seem on the air," Anita claims.

When I asked my listeners to show up at a McDonald's or a shopping mall to watch a radio show, they did it. Large numbers of people did what I suggested, and that's when I realized my listeners were not only fans of the music, they were *my* fans too. In radio it's called a "following" and sadly, sometimes, it became a scary thing.

We all know what "fan" is short for.

12

1982 was the year of the stalker. I used to joke around and say, "You're nobody 'til somebody stalks you," but now I don't think it's so funny. When you're on the radio you want a following. You ask your listeners to come to every event and you begin to recognize some of them after a while. I was picking up some extra cash by hosting a weekly dance party and, even though I knew better, one night I accepted a Quaalude from a listener. At closing time I was stumbling to my car when I faced my stalker for the first time. He was the same guy I'd vaguely seen at other WMMR events and I was pretty sure he was wearing the exact same T-shirt. Suddenly I was fighting him off as I tried to get into my car and next practically drove over him while trying to leave.

But was he really a threat or was it the Quaalude? I hated myself for not knowing what the fuck really happened.

I started receiving letters at the radio station from someone who was very troubled. There was talk of telekinesis and drawings of blood-dripping knives. I took them to my program director who noticed that the letters also included crazy talk about killing me, Debbie Harry (the lead singer from the band Blondie), and President Ronald Reagan. He called the FBI.

Soon after, my father answered the phone in the middle of the night and the man on the other end told him I was a sex slave in a prostitution ring. I'm sure my dad relived that "your daughter is in a Mexican prison" phone call and wondered how this could be happening yet again. He probably also decided to finally get an unlisted phone number. Luckily my ever-trusting father took notes and called me to relay all the information, including the stalker's name, which was Ed. I didn't know it, but a few days later the stalker showed up at the radio station and applied for an internship. According to the guard who was very excited to now have something to guard, the stalker started sleeping in Rittenhouse Square at night. I had to walk from my apartment through the park every morning at about nine-thirty but I didn't know I was in danger. The FBI came to the radio station and after a short discussion it was very obvious they only cared about protecting the President who was scheduled to be in Philly soon. The station's general manager got involved and called the police.

The Philadelphia Police Department has a sex crimes unit. I got a call from an Officer Guzzy and he explained how we were going to try to catch my stalker. After my shift ended at 2 P.M. we would drive around Rittenhouse Square in an unmarked police car. If I thought I saw someone resembling Ed, I'd get out of the car, and walk slowly. Then just as Ed jumped out of the bushes and tried to kill me, Officer Guzzy would hypothetically show up just in the nick of time.

Unfortunately we didn't see Ed again until he showed up at my apartment building a week later. I almost walked right into him. I screamed at the top of my lungs. The doorman ran out of the mailroom and Ed took off into the park. Officer Guzzy was called and he finally made an arrest that night after finding Ed sleeping on a bench. My dad and I had to go to the jail to meet with the judge. Ed somehow passed his psycho test and was really angry when he was led into the room. Still handcuffed, red in the face, and loudly yelling at me, Ed was pissing off the judge. I stood very still and tried not to look over at my stalker as the judge tried to figure out what was going on. When he asked me if I knew what Ed wanted from me I answered that I felt he wanted to kill me along with the President of the United States and Debbie Harry.

"Who?, the judge asked.

"Blondie, your honor," I said, trying not to laugh. My stalker thought it was hilarious and when he wouldn't stop laughing they took him out of the room. Still, somehow, he was released a couple of days later but he had a court date and I really thought he would be put away. My parents and I were about to park our car near City Hall when I believe I saw Ed getting on a bus with a suitcase. He never came into the courtroom and the case was never heard. I never saw or heard from him again.

In June I interviewed Asia, a "super group" that was made up of Steve Howe and Geoff Downes formerly of Yes; John Wetton from King Crimson, Roxy Music, Wishbone Ash, and Uriah Heep among other bands; and Carl Palmer from The Crazy World of Arthur Brown and Emerson Lake

& Palmer. Their manager, Brian Lane, was Yes's manager. He changed his name to Brian after Brian Epstein, who managed the Beatles. John Kalodner, their A&R guy, was also a huge player in the music world. He signed Foreigner, AC/DC, and Peter Gabriel among many others. John was a big hero of the guys in Aerosmith, Jimmy Page and Sammy

Hagar.

Carl Palmer and I were instantly attracted to each other. After the interview in Philly, he called me and I agreed to meet him in Norfolk, Virginia.

I landed at the Norfolk airport and someone picked me up and drove me to the venue where the band was already onstage. I was standing on the side of the stage when Carl Palmer saw me and smiled. After the show we boarded a plane to Atlanta. Travelling with very rich rock stars was fun and Carl made me laugh. We both liked to wear really short shorts and go jogging. He looked very healthy and was drug-free but he did have a few odd turn-ons. For example, Carl liked me to sit underneath the stage under the drum kit during the show, as if I was in between his legs. For me it was like a giant MRI but I didn't say anything because I knew he liked it.

I hoped being alone with Carl would be worth the flight. I wasn't disappointed. Carl had the body of a much younger man. We had the kind of sex I had when I was much younger—hot, hard, and fast. Carl seemed to explode inside me and it wiped him out like the end of one of his crashing drum solos. I felt powerful.

I was surprised when Carl told me about his personal life and showed me the photos of his family in his wallet. He said he missed his home in the Canary Islands and beamed when he showed me a picture of his car, a Rolls-Royce Silver Cloud. I'm not saying it turned me off, but I was over it by the time we got to Atlanta. Asia's fans were rabid and they acted like Asia were the Beatles. There was lots of screaming and crying and one of the fans grabbed me by my hair when I was trying to get into the limo. Carl was a charming man and I had fun with him, but I was glad to get back to Philly and my radio show.

On July 24, Billy Squier was opening for Queen at the Spectrum. He came to the radio station for an interview and the room seemed to heat up when he slid next to me at the microphone. Billy was the hot video darling of MTV and he had a crazy look in his eyes that promised, *I'm*

going to rock your world. He flirted with me during the interview and then invited me to dinner before his show. At the Cuban restaurant on South Street we made out in front of the gawking customers. I could tell they knew who he was. Or maybe they recognized me. I wasn't sure but I didn't care. I went home just long enough to change my clothes before heading off to the Spectrum. I invited Jessica Velmans to join me and we stood on the stage and screamed "Stroke Me" into the microphone. I sure hope it wasn't on.

After the show, I couldn't wait to get Billy alone. I thought we'd set the bed on fire and he'd put those moves on me that I saw in his videos. When we were finally alone in his hotel room, we started to rip off each other's clothes. I was about to explode when he started to work his way *down there*. *Oh yeah*, I thought, *he's really good at this*. After about fifteen minutes I was beginning to think he wasn't going to stop. And I was right. Billy didn't seem to want to do anything else. I tried to guide him toward my face but no amount of pulling on his arms or trying to lift his head did any good. He just wouldn't stop. It would have been funny if it wasn't so painful. He didn't stop and I couldn't believe it. Billy finally fell asleep and I was never more grateful for anything in my life.

In the morning I could barely walk. I hurt so bad I could only move my lower body if I walked very slowly. I took a taxi to the radio station. I was slowly trying to get out of the backseat when I saw my general manager standing at the curb. He gave me a look that said, *What happened to you? And aren't those the same clothes you were wearing yesterday?* but he was far too much of a gentleman to mention it aloud. He pretended not to notice that I had to limp into the elevator.

There's a lesson to be learned somewhere in this story but I don't know what it is.

I needed to take a vacation. On July 29, Jessica and I were off to Greece for two weeks in beautiful Mykonos. The Greek men we met were exactly what we each needed. Jessica met a guy who literally took her away from everything she knew. She said something to me about his ranch in the hills, and I didn't see much of her for the first week. I met "Adonis" at a disco that played Foreigner's "Urgent" over and over. He didn't speak English but between the loud music and his loud motorcycle, it didn't matter. There's nothing like sizzling summer sex in paradise. I was a happy girl with a rockin' life. I looked forward to going back to Philly, playing my music on the radio for my listeners, going to concerts, and partying with the fun people that I met. It was exciting not knowing what was going to happen next. This was the life for me. No ties to anyone. No more early mornings.

On September 19, I returned from a dinner to celebrate Rosh Hashana with my parents. When I checked my answering machine there were nine phone messages. They were all from Warren Zevon

"Hello Anita? It's Warren. . . Zevon. I'm on your coast and hope you'll call me back." *Beep.*

"Anita, it's Warren again. . . Just wanted to make sure I left you my number." *Beep.*

"Hi, it's Warren. I'll just keep calling you until I reach you so don't bother calling me." *Beep.*

"Guess who? Okay, I'm pretty sure you're not there, so I'll call again. Did I leave my number?" *Beep.*

I didn't even get to listen to the last few messages before Warren called again. When I answered the phone he seemed tongue-tied for a second.

"Hello, Anita?" he growled.

"Hi, yes, I'm here." I was breathless.

My mind was racing with questions I didn't want to ask. Where was the wife and what about the girlfriend? I had to know. Warren was fine with my questions and told me that he was divorced and no longer lived with his girlfriend. We decided we should be together and I packed a bag and got on a plane.

It seemed a little *too* easy.

Warren's "Into the Finland Station" tour started on September 21, 1982. George Gruel was the road manager/bus driver and the bus was on loan from Rick Springfield. George hired a local band to play with Warren, after hearing them perform in an Orange County strip mall. They were a Zevon cover band, called Z Deluxe, and they had never been on the road, or anywhere else.

I joined them in New Haven, Connecticut and Warren and I spent all day and night in his room. I was transported to another dimension during sex. It felt natural and surreal at the same time. I could have flown back to Philly without a plane. I admitted to Warren that I was crushed when I moved to Los Angeles and couldn't see him. He told me that would never happen again and I believed him. Unlike all the other times, I didn't feel like it wasn't just happening to me. It was about "us" from the very beginning. That was how Warren was. When he loved you, you knew it and it felt wonderful.

Warren wanted me to know about all the things that he loved. It was important to him that I could tell the difference between the music of the classical composers, especially Bartok, Shostakovich, and Stravinsky. When we discovered I shared my 25th of March birthday with Bartok, Warren seemed proud. He wanted me to understand the great works of writers James Joyce and Thomas Pynchon and he read them over and over again. I started reading mystery novels by Ross MacDonald and Robert B. Parker. We did all the stupid things that new couples do. We had nicknames for each other. He was "Mac" and I was "Sally" because Warren thought I looked like Susan St. James from TV's *MacMillan and Wife*, one of our favorites. He called me "Lil' Possum", but I never understood why. I could stay in a hotel room with Warren forever. Give me a bag of pot and some room service and that's all I needed. We would watch the same movie over and over. I must have seen *The Wrath of Khan* in every city. Life on the road with Warren was actually better than my life on the radio at WMMR. For the first time, I didn't need to take a break. I didn't want to go home.

13

Warren and I were sitting in my apartment in the La Chateau building on Rittenhouse Square when he told me he wanted to move in with me. I was surprised and caught off guard. Warren saw the look on my face before I had time to mask it. He winced and his smile disappeared. I spent the next three hours convincing him that I wanted him to move in with me. I think I convinced him but I wasn't sure I believed it. I was truly in love with Warren but I also knew that if he moved in everything could change. Now it would just be the two of us.

I wondered if he was running away from L.A. and everyone who tried to get him to stop drinking. When Warren wasn't on the road with a show to do and another to prepare for there was too much free time. I could hang out and stay pretty stoned yet coherent but Warren couldn't. Unless he was performing or recording, his drinking was out of control. He took too many pills, smoked too many cigarettes, and drank amazing amounts of vodka. His choice was Stolichnaya, which I learned was not the name of a classical composer. I was clueless about alcoholism, but I knew that Warren's capacity for vodka was ridiculous. I convinced him to move in because I loved him and I was also flattered. But I privately crossed my fingers and took a deep breath. Maybe things would work out if we stayed on the road most of the time.

I decided to leave WMMR. I quit my job so I could go on the road with Warren full-time. I knew how I met Warren and I understood he called me to go on tour with him because Kim wouldn't go. If I didn't want him to move on without me, I had to be there. I would be the supportive girlfriend on the road. Warren was worth it.

On Sept 27 Warren appeared on *Late Night with David Letterman* for the first time. We both worshipped Dave. We were somewhere in some hotel room when we got the call from Paul Shaffer. Paul needed music charts for the songs Warren wanted to perform on the show. This should have been a happy time but it seems that Kim Lankford was also trying to join the tour. George Gruel had done all he could to keep Kim and Warren from a showdown on the phone and she decided to find out why.

Kim obviously had no idea that I was with Warren and he refused to deal with anything but the *Letterman* appearance. I kept asking him why he hadn't told Kim what was really happening. He wouldn't answer me so I got mad and went home. When I arrived at 30th Street Station I picked up a *Philadelphia Inquirer* and the latest *People* magazine. I got home and fell on the bed. I was thumbing through *People* when I saw an article with the headline: AFTER A LONG BOUT WITH BOOZE, ROCKER WARREN ZEVON GETS HIGH (AND DRY) WITH ACTRESS KIM LANKFOrd. The November 8, 1982 Couples column was devoted to *Knots Landing*'s Kim Lankford and her fiancé rocker Warren Zevon. Warren is quoted in the article. He says Kim acts as his "salvation, his reminder of how nice life can be." Kim is described as "tanned and barefoot". The article claims "they aim to wed someday, on the Montana ranch of their novelist friend Tom McGuane."

I was barely able to breathe. After watching Warren's appearance on *Letterman*, I was almost ready to forgive him. He and Dave had a great chemistry and I loved *that* Warren. The one on TV. Warren called and I told him about the *People* magazine article.

"Oh, that," he grimaced. "Don't pay any attention to that, honey. It was written about six weeks ago."

I never expected him to say something like that and I had no response. It was sort of funny, really, and I *did* want to be with him. He promised to deal with his former life when we got to L.A. I said okay and Warren and I had make up phone sex.

On Oct 1, 1982 we started the Into the Finland Station—Part 2 tour

Warren's tour took him to a different city almost every night. It was a grueling schedule but we were having a blast. I thought my radio career would suffer, but in fact, I was in demand. There was a new rock radio station in Philadelphia called WYSP. I was getting calls from its new program director, Michael Picozzi, who I worked with when we were at WMMR. I kept putting off the call back. But Picozzi wasn't going to give up. We finally met for lunch and he dangled a deal in front of me. I listened but didn't agree to anything and flew to Los Angeles with Warren. We checked into the Sunset Marquis on November

17 and stayed until December 2. When Warren and I checked into a hotel room we immediately did a couple of things. He'd call for more towels and I would move some of the furniture around to make it more bearable, if everything wasn't nailed down. I could have my space and he could create Warren's world. Warren got drunk and then he called Kim and tried to explain things to her. She was mad and I felt bad for her. I thought she loved Warren. I was glad she had her acting career and TV show. It made me realize I should have a job too so I called Picozzi and said yes to WYSP.

On December 9 the station issued a press release:

ANITA IS BACK AND READY TO ROCK ON 94 WYSP!

Philly's favorite daughter
returns to the radio
Thursday, December 16 in
her favorite spot, 10 A.M. to

2 P.M. on 94 WYSP. Anita Gevinson (please no last name) will be playing the best music and have a forum for those outrageous stories and problems that we've learned to love. WYSP's Program Director, Michael Picozzi, feels Anita is one of the best things that has happened to YSP in recent history. "Anita's not just a DJ," explained Picozzi, "she's a genuine personality and 'Philly' through and through. In an industry that has

discouraged anything but

boredom, it's a pleasure to

work with a genuine radio

star. Besides, she makes

me laugh."

It felt great to be back with the listeners who, to my

surprise, made the switch from WMMR

I had to come up with a "noon feature" for WYSP

to go up against the "workforce blocks" (three songs from

one artist by request from a job site) that started on my

watch on WMMR. Michael Picozzi was standing in the

studio one afternoon trying to talk to me about something while I was busy answering the phones. I tried to keep my conversations short so I answered every question with a couple of words. Michael listened to me giving advice to the guy whose girlfriend cheated on him and then wanted to hear a Bon Jovi song. Then he heard me yell at a girl who asked where she could meet a rich guy. He laughed as I told her she would regret being a gold digger.

"How do you do this?" he asked

"What do you think I do while the music is playing?" I teased as I took a hit from a burning joint.

"You should do this on the air," Michael said. "We'll call it 'Ask Anita'."

Before I could say anything, Michael went into the studio and recorded an opening for the show. He found some soap opera organ music and used a Don Pardo delivery: "Time now for Ask Anita on 94 WYSP."

Thereafter, every day from noon until one o clock, I took calls and gave relationship advice. It was easy for me, and the ratings went through the roof. The fact that I was in a dysfunctional relationship made it even stranger that I felt I could tell everyone else what to do.

On weekends I started to join Warren on the road again.

We were back at the Sunset Marquis on January 20. This time we had a reason to get out of bed. Warren was appearing at the Roxy and I was planning to sit in the girlfriend box. The shows brought out all the L.A. music stars, like J.D. Souther, who Warren loved like a brother. Eric Burdon, who I'd seen so many years ago with the Animals in Atlantic City, came backstage after the show. Even Bruce Springsteen got on his motorcycle and drove over to the Roxy. I stood by the side door and waited for him to drive into the parking lot. Bruce looked at me and wasn't sure if he knew me or not. I just smiled and led him upstairs to the dressing rooms.

On February 11, 1983 an article by Gail Shister ran in the *Philadelphia Inquirer*. It featured me and "Ask Anita". The headline read: SHE LOVES TO TALK TO UNSEEN LISTENERS.

> Confused by Cupid? Lost
>
> in Love? Hung up on
>
> heartache? Then just tune
>
> your dial to WYSP and

"Ask Anita", local radio-land's answer to Ann Landers. Anita's advice to the lovelorn hour, at noon, on weekdays, began about six weeks ago. The response has been heartwarming. The station is adding four more telephone lines to its present three to accommodate the noon rush hour. To date, Anita has taken a total of 400 calls on the air. The age range is 13 to 39, the bulk of them are between 16 and 23. The majority are men. Anita, an animated Lilliputian in black capri pants and high heels takes the show seriously. "A young guy called and said he was raised Catholic and met a girl who was into black magic. He said they were in a ceremony at his house where they got naked and drank blood. His dad walked in and freaked out. He wanted to know if he should make up with his father or go to Africa with his girlfriend. I told him to talk to his dad." As for her own love life, Anita is in a

long distance romance

with rock star Warren

Zevon. Each weekend

they rendezvous in

whatever city he's

performing. It's an

expensive way to be in

love but Anita thinks it's

worth it.

On February 21 Warren and I were in New York at the

Berkshire Place Hotel on East 52nd Street. Warren had a

show at The Bottom Line and was talking about how much

he hoped Martin Scorsese would come. Warren's

"Werewolves of London" was part of the soundtrack for

the movie *The Color of Money*. They met once when

Warren was with Kim. It was difficult for me to hear from

the *Knots Landing* fans showing up at Warren's shows. When they saw me get off the bus instead of Kim someone would routinely say, *"You're* not Kim Lankford." I wanted to do something that Kim would do, so I looked in Warren's phone book and I called Martin Scorsese's office. I spoke to an assistant who said he would pass the invitation along to Mr. Scorsese. Warren was thrilled when Scorsese showed up and brought actor Jeff Bridges with him. It was a great night and so far Warren was staying sober.

On March 17, 1983 Warren proposed to me while we were having sex in a hotel room in Dallas. I said yes but swore to myself that I'd find an alternative to the traditional wedding. I loved Warren but I didn't think we needed to get married. I always thought I was too evolved for that. I begged him not to tell my parents about our engagement until we planned it ourselves. He ignored me and one night before dinner at my parents' condo, he asked my dad for my hand in marriage. My mom cried. I begged her to keep it a secret and she did for a while.

Warren began his Live at Least tour part 3. At the end of April, Warren went to Hawaii and took his son Jordan with him. I wasn't there but I knew that Warren had started drinking again. I started to feel sad for Warren and how much he needed to drink. He could guzzle a whole fifth of vodka and not be drunk. I hated myself for thinking of reverting to the same cut and run plan I always used when things got tough. I wanted to help Warren but I didn't know what to do.

"Honey, why are you drinking so much?" I finally asked. "What would make you feel better?"

"I need to see my kids," he said to my surprise. "I want to see more of Jordan, and my daughter Ariel is in Paris and I haven't seen her in three years".

"Okay," I heard myself saying,"we'll send for your kids."

It was easier said than done. In fact it was very complicated. Warren couldn't understand why his ex-wife took Ariel to Paris. There were a couple of angry letters exchanged and when we sent them a cassette player so Ariel could hear Warren's music, her mother taped her saying things like "I don't have a daddy. He doesn't love me," and sent the cassette to us. I thought Warren was going to go insane. He was angry and in obvious pain whenever he spoke about his daughter. In April Warren had a couple of shows in Hawaii and he convinced his son's mother to let Jordan go with him. Jordan's mother seemed to me to be a lovely woman who honestly wanted her son to be around his father.

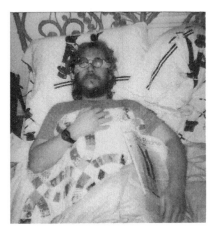

When Warren returned, he resumed drinking and I didn't know how to help him. I was relieved when he was offered a summer European tour. Trying to stay sober, trying to write music, trying not to resent me for being able to go to work each day, it was too much for Warren. I understood but didn't know how to help him. When I asked him what he wanted me to do he would say, "Cook a big dinner"

We could have holed up and made tuna melts forever but I saw Warren sliding away in a sea of vodka. I had to make excuses for him and cancel planned rehearsal and recording sessions with local band The Hooters and Dave Stewart of Eurythmics. He tried but couldn't beat his addiction and I was afraid he would die, just like my sister.

He said we shouldn't be together since I refused to learn anything about his disease. I gave him a look that made him leave the apartment for the first time in weeks. He checked into the Barclay Hotel right across the square for a change of scenery. I was grateful. Life with Warren was exhausting. The next day he came home with a song called "Reconsider Me".

One day on my way home from work, I picked up my copy of *Rolling Stone* magazine with the other mail and tossed it to Warren on the couch. When he got to the Random Notes section he let out a scream.

"What the fuck?" he yelled. "Honey, look at this."

There it was, a blurb about Warren being dropped by his record label. That's how he found out. He was devastated. After ten or fifteen minutes of bitter hateful spewing aimed at everyone he ever knew, Warren went into the bedroom and slammed the door. I don't think I saw him for four or five days. What would we do about the European tour? We decided to do what any ready to explode and meltdown couple does when things get tough. They go on the road. They get on a plane and fly far away. We decided that no one had to know how bad off Warren was. He was in debt with no record label, no tour support, no band, no road manager, no new songs, and drinking heavily. I asked my patient program director for the time off and he, as always, said okay. We got a letter from Warren's ex asking us to pick up Ariel at a boarding school outside of Paris. We somehow agreed to do it without making sure we had the address of the school. Warren was freaking out about every bad thing that could happen.

"Nothing's bad luck is it?" Warren would ask me over and over again.

I tried to ignore all of my gut instincts and stayed busy packing. I had my hair cut at the trendy hair salon next door to our apartment. The guy cut it a little shorter than I liked but it looked good and would be easy to care for. Warren hated it. He threw a fit like a two-year-old. He screamed about what he'd like to do to the hairdresser and I was shocked to see how long he carried on. I stood there for a minute trying to figure out who he reminded me of. It was my sister.

The new road manager, Ron Moss, flew into Philly to meet us. I thought he was too straight and he obviously had no idea what he was getting himself into. As we got into the taxi on the way to the airport I noticed a lot of policemen standing around the hair salon. We drove by and I saw that all the windows had been smashed. *Well there goes the*

neighborhood, I thought. Years later, Warren confessed to me that he was the one who broke all the windows because he hated my haircut. I don't know if I would have gotten on that plane had I known that.

We arrived at Heathrow Airport on June 22 and checked into the Montcalm Hotel on Great Cumberland Place in London. Warren played at Dingwalls at Camden

Lock on the 24th. The show didn't start until 11:30 P.M. and Warren struggled to stay sober all day. On the 25th we were in Belfast, Ireland at McMordi Hall, Queens University. Next it was back to the Montcalm for a couple of days off, followed by a concert at Hammersmith Odeon on the 29th. On the 30th we were in Hamburg, Germany and on July 1 Warren performed at the Roskilde Festival in Denmark. The line-up was The Scabs, John Cale & Band, Warren, Eurythmics, Simple Minds, U2, Peter Gabriel, and Van Morrison closed the show.

Most of the same bands travelled to the Torhout and Werchter Festivals in Belgium. We had a day off in Brussels, then we were off to Amsterdam for a show at the Paradiso.

In Dublin Warren finally lost it when someone in the audience shouted something he didn't want to hear. He stopped the show and offered refunds. The promoter was not amused. By that time Warren was drinking heavily and I was not sure how he continued to perform. By the time we got to Cork I wanted to go home but I knew that wasn't possible. I hoped being reunited with his daughter would make Warren decide to stop drinking.

After the tour mercifully ended we flew to Geneva and rented a car. We would pick up Ariel and fly back to

Philly together. Warren was drunk and so I had to drive to Chamonix. I watched and listened carefully as the car rental guy drew a line on a map from the Geneva airport to Chamonix. Two hours later I cried "uncle" and pulled into the next place I saw—ironically a bar. I went in and left a passed out Warren in the car. I opened my map on the bar and showed them where I wanted to go. The man smiled and said something in French. I said I didn't understand so he said it again. He pointed to a place on the map that seemed very far from my red-circled Chamonix. I decided to drive until I found a hotel and call it a night. About a half hour later I found a hotel in a very dark little town. Warren woke up and we staggered inside. In the morning I was astounded to learn that we were in fact in Chamonix. Divine intervention? Who knows? At least there was an intervention of some sort. We were so happy until we realized we didn't have the address of Ariel's school. The letter with that info arrived a couple of days after we left Philly.

For the next three days we knocked on every door until we found Ariel, who had been packed and waiting the whole time. It was heartbreaking for the first few minutes because Ariel didn't recognize her father, who had grown a beard. She had no idea who I was. We had to sit down and talk with the headmaster before he let us take her. Afterward we walked out to the car and Warren dropped Ariel's suitcase by the trunk and ran around to open the door for her. I slid into the backseat and Warren ran around the front of the car, got in behind the wheel, put the car in reverse, and ran over the suitcase. Ariel turned to me and said, "*That's* my dad." I cracked up and Warren started laughing as he squinted and drove away.

We spent a couple days in the hotel and Warren was
toasting his happiness too much. He was barely coherent
and I had to get us out of there. We missed our TWA flight

from Heathrow and had to switch to a British Airways flight, which we also almost missed. On the flight back to Philly, Warren sat by himself in the back of the plane and got drunk while Ariel and I sat in the middle of the plane and watched a movie. Upon arrival, Ariel's acclimation was anything but instant. At first, she wanted to keep her clothes in her suitcase and she would only eat pizza or fried chicken. I had to reassure Ariel that her mother was going to return for her. But after about a week Ariel seemed fine and adjusted. Things were pretty normal, for us anyway.

One day Warren let Ariel watch a horror movie and when it got too scary he panicked. He beat himself up about it for days. Warren tried to stop drinking all day but now he slept all the time. I had no choice; I had to take Ariel to work with me. She sat on my lap as I played the music and gave advice on "Ask Anita". Ariel drew pictures and never said a word while the microphone was on. Warren slowly started getting it together. He received a call from Stevie

Nicks's people asking him to open for her in Pittsburgh on July 23. Ariel and I flew up to the gig so she could see her dad perform for the first time. We had seats in the middle of the theatre. The people sitting around us were getting restless for the show to start. They started chanting and clapping in unison. Ariel wondered what was going on. Finally, Warren took the stage and when the crowd went wild I turned to Ariel and she smiled proudly.

In August, for Ariel's seventh birthday, I took her to the local Bloomingdale's on Old York Road in Jenkintown. She picked out a pair of grey and pink Nike sneakers. Warren and I took her to the local dinner theatre to see *Annie*. It was a wonderful day and even though Warren had too much to drink he got weepy instead of angry. Still, we were doing things like a family and I was starting to believe we could be happy. Warren and I moved into a bigger apartment in the same building. It overlooked Rittenhouse square and had wall-to-wall mirrors in the living and dining room. And, even more importantly, two bedrooms. After the "Summer of the Kids", Warren turned the second bedroom into a recording studio.

When Warren went back on the road for a couple of gigs I took Ariel to the Jersey Shore to visit my parents. They'd rented a little apartment in Surf City on Long Beach Island. Jessica Velmans came down from New York and we walked on the beach and giggled about how maternal I had become.

My parents loved spending time with Ariel. At six years old she was as funny and smart as she was pretty. My mother took her to the Franklin Institute and tried to answer her many questions about everything. We went to the library across the street from the apartment where Ariel got a library card. When I took her hand to cross the street, she joked "Not so hard, you're not taking me to jail!"

Warren's son Jordan accompanied him home from L.A. and the two half-siblings got to spend time together for the first time in over three years. Jordan was a joy to be around and he seemed to be impressed with my job on the radio. He and Ariel got along great and the apartment was full of laughter. It made a fun if somewhat chaotic household yet Warren hung in there and really enjoyed himself. Nonetheless I'm sure he was fighting the urge to drink himself into oblivion.

Eventually Jordan returned to his mom in L.A. and Warren's ex came to pick up Ariel. It was a bittersweet reunion and regrettably things got ugly. There was a loud argument in Rittenhouse Square about whether the ex should stick around for a couple of days. Warren wasn't having it. They ended up pushing each other's buttons and then Warren pushed her, literally. She left and we didn't talk about her again. The apartment was too quiet once the kids left and Warren retreated into the second bedroom. He turned it into a studio but couldn't write anything except new words to Bob Dylan's "Gotta Serve Somebody". I tried to make him see how sick he was. I was afraid to leave him when I had to go to work and, equally telling, afraid to return.

14

My mother finally spilled the beans about my engagement to Warren while she was having her hair done. The woman who owned the hair salon had a son who worked for *The Trenton Times*. He broke the story in a small blurb. Gail Shister, from the *Philadelphia Inquirer*, saw it and called me. She pumped me for information and I started lying. But I had no choice. I couldn't explain to *anyone* why I didn't think Warren and I should get married. I couldn't say that I never wanted to marry anyone and had no interest in being a wife. I couldn't say that Warren shouldn't get married to anyone ever again. And I wasn't going to deal with my fear that Warren would end up like my sister.

On September 14, the headline of the TV/Radio Talk section of the *Philadelphia Inquirer* read A WEDDING QUESTION TO 'ASK ANITA'.

> Anita Gevinson, rock disc
>
> jockey queen at WYSP-
>
> FM and adviser to the
>
> lovelorn during her daily
>
> 'Ask Anita' call-in hour,
>
> might do well to
>
> contemplate this
>
> brainteaser: When is a
>
> wedding not a wedding?
>
> The answer of course is
>
> when the wedding belongs

to Gevinson, 31, and her rock 'n' roll roommate, Warren Zevon, 36. These two have gone through more nuptial permutations than Liz and Dick—except for the fact that Gevinson and Zevon have yet to tie the knot. He's been married twice before; she has yet to take the plunge—and therein lies the tale. "We've talked about marriage, but haven't set a date," says Gevinson, who has dated her intended off and on since 1976. "We started to plan a wedding, but the

guest list got so big, we

would have had to print

backstage passes and hire

security. Then we decided

to wait. Then we almost

got married secretly in

Europe, but it would have

cheated our families out of

a wedding. In the

meantime we're calling

ourselves engaged."

On November 13 an article appeared in the Inklings

section of the *Philadelphia Inquirer*. Tim Whitaker wrote

the headline WARREN ZEVON: YO, ANITA-I LOVE YA!

A match made in rock 'n'

roll heaven—that's what

they're calling our town's

torrid love affair between rock star Warren Zevon and Anita Gevinson of WYSP-FM. After being introduced by Anita before a recent SRO crowd at the Brandywine Club in Chadds Ford recently, Warren launched into a hyped-up version of Buddy Holly's "Not Fade Away" that began with the singer sliding across the floor on his knees in front of a mini-skirted (and slightly embarrassed) Anita. Said Warren: "There's a certain Philadelphia girl I've been

in love with for a long, long

time and tonight's my night

to show it."

After the tour ended, Warren came home and stayed

there. I didn't know how to help him stop drinking and we

tiptoed around each other

for weeks.

Like a knight in

shining armor, Warren's

true friend J.D. Souther

showed up on a snowy day.

To be fair, maybe J.D. was the only one Warren called. J.D.

was in New York working on his album *Home by Dawn*

and took a train to Philly. J.D. is a brilliant songwriter, and

he and Warren had known each other for years. They

laughed a lot which was great to hear. I had forgotten how

much Warren and I used to laugh. I missed the romantic,

funny Warren. One night we went out to dinner at one of

our favorite restaurants, Friday, Saturday, Sunday on 21st Street. Halfway through the meal, Warren asked J.D. to be the best man at our wedding. When he agreed, Warren poured some champagne in our glasses. They both turned and looked at me and I just sat there and tried to smile. I couldn't look either of them in the eye and no one made a toast. I would go to bed and leave Warren and J.D. in the living room where they would sit for the next three hours playing the same song, "She's About a Mover" by Sir Douglas Quintet. It didn't seem like they were doing any songwriting, but by the time J.D. left, he and Warren had written "Trouble Waiting to Happen". Somehow I knew how true that was.

I gave Warren a subscription to *The Ring* magazine for his birthday. I've watched boxing matches with my dad since I was a kid. I told Warren about the "Boom Boom Mancini vs. Doo Koo Kim" fight which ended with Boom Boom killing Doo Koo. He was fascinated by the story and we started to watch boxing matches together. In January of 1984 I was scheduled to appear on an annual telethon, which aired on one of the local TV stations. That same night Boom Boom was returning to the ring to fight Bobby Chacon. I hoped to be back in time to watch but the telethon was running behind schedule. I called Warren and asked him to tape the fight for me. He ended the call by saying "Hurry home honey. Hurry on home." When I got in he'd written the song "Boom Boom Mancini". Warren also wrote this piece of music for me.

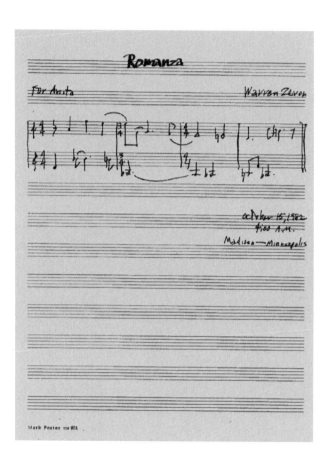

As a DJ I was given a lot of promotional items from the record companies. When Warren first moved in I folded up my life-size cardboard cutout of Elvis Costello and took my Billy Squier gold record to the radio station. When we moved into a bigger apartment, I felt that Warren was secure enough to handle a poster of Prince hanging in the second bathroom.

"That has to go," Warren laughed as he stared at Prince wearing nothing but black bikini bottoms.

"I love Prince," I said, hoping he wouldn't leave me for saying that.

Instead Warren started to love Prince, too—at least his music. He even recorded a cover of "Raspberry Beret" with the guys from R.E.M.

The Hindu Love Gods sessions would never have happened without a guy named Andy Slater and my love of the band. It's hard to imagine but in 1984 R.E.M. was only four years old. They had released two albums, *Murmur* and *Reckoning*, and they had yet to break out of their cult status. I was an early fan but Warren had never heard of them. Andy Slater went to college with the members of R.E.M. in Athens, Georgia and was a fan of Warren's. Andy worked for Virgin Records at the time and thought of the idea to put Warren together with R.E.M. Michael Stipe, R.E.M.'s lead singer, wasn't around so Warren would be the lead singer and band leader. Warren wasn't initially sold on the idea and asked me what I thought. I was thrilled for two reasons. I thought they would sound great together and it was something for Warren to do. He left for Athens with no idea what was in store. I was finally home alone and loving it. Warren would call every couple hours and tell me how cold it was and how young the band was and how they had to borrow a drum kit and drive it to the studio themselves. He was mostly just amused and loved playing the music he loved with a willing band of great musicians.

Warren didn't expect anything to happen after *The Hindu Love Gods* session. But Andy Slater called again and told Warren that Virgin Records wanted to sign him.

Now if he could only get sober.

One day I returned home after work and found Warren in his overcoat standing next to a couple of suitcases.

"I called my cousin, Dr. Sandy," Warren said in a soft faraway voice. "He's going to meet me and get me into detox."

I couldn't look at him. "Where are you going?" was all I could say.

"I'll call and let you know. I have to go now." Warren was almost whispering.

I simply nodded. He leaned over and kissed me on the top of my head and left.

I had no idea where Warren was. I thought Dr. Sandy was a dentist who lived in upstate New York. The apartment was so quiet and it felt so strange. I didn't know if I liked being there alone or not. I got a phone call a couple of days after Warren left and a man from a hospital called St Mary's in Minnesota told me I needed to fly there and be part of Warren's treatment. I didn't want to go. *It's not my problem*, I said to myself. *I'm not the addict.* I packed a bag and made sure I had enough pot to take to rehab. Besides my parents, I only told my fellow DJ Debbi Calton where I was going and she kept it to herself. I lied to my program director and got on a plane.

I didn't know a lot about rehab, but I knew I thought it was bullshit. When you're in the hospital, it's not reality. Everyone has time for everything you need to say, even if it's always all about you. The transferring of addictions starts to occur. How will too much coffee and cigarettes help you become a disciplined person? How are you expected to go back into a cold world where no one cares what you've been through? Maybe if it took longer than a couple of weeks to "conquer" the addiction, I'd buy into it. Sitting in a smoke-filled room hopped up on caffeine just doesn't seem like effective treatment.

When I arrived at the hospital I wasn't permitted to see Warren. They wouldn't let us be in the same "group" for three days. In the meantime I had two daily group sessions with the other "co-dependents". I sat in a circle with men and women of all ages and lifestyles and listened to one horror story after another.

"My name is Pete and I'm married to Mary and there hadn't been any physical violence in our marriage for three months, before two weeks ago."

"I'm Sandy and my husband Tim still won't take a vacation and I'm still afraid of him sometimes. He has a terrible temper when he drinks."

Then it was my turn.

"My name is Anita and my boyfriend's name is Warren."

I was interrupted by Pete, who said, "You're not married?"

"No," I answered, not sure where this was going.

"Do you have kids?" Pete wanted to know.

"No," I said again.

"See that door?" Pete said, adamantly pointing to it. "Run as fast as you can and don't look back."

I couldn't believe what he just said. That settled it. I was not going to do this. I thought of my sister again and how no matter what we did and how much we loved her she couldn't be saved. I recalled what my sister's death did to my parents. I was sure Warren would eventually die too and they loved Warren. I couldn't let it happen again. I imagined the story in *Rolling Stone* about how Warren survived everything except living with the DJ from Philly.

We were finally allowed to be in the same room, Warren was the star of the group. There was nothing anonymous about his alcoholism. When it was my turn to speak I lost control and let it all out. I said I didn't understand why everybody in the room was so fucking happy. I said I thought it was the lowest point of my life and couldn't understand how they didn't also feel that way. Then I dropped the bomb. I said I didn't want Warren to come back to Philly with me. He got up and ran out of the room. The others just stared at me with a look that said "Die bitch."

"So what do you want me to do? Who should I call for Warren?" the shocked counselor asked me.

"Call Jackson Browne," I answered and then I got up and walked out.

I found Warren in his room sitting on his bed holding one of my T-shirts that he'd kept underneath his pillow. We both started crying and I couldn't say anything so I got up and walked out. I packed up my stuff and flew home. I felt like the worst person in the world.

Warren came to Philly a couple of months later and got his stuff. We hardly spoke and I couldn't look at him. I went back to work and told no one what had happened. Everyone found out that we had broken up but no one asked why.

In September I was asked to be the morning D.J. at WYSP. I decided to do it and just get over the whole early morning issue. This time I had some help. I worked with newsman Gary Lee Horn, funny guy R.D. Steele (who did a variety of voices and wrote crazy skits), and a producer named Bob Panaccio.

On October 24, 1984 the morning show and I were featured in a *Philadelphia Daily News* article by Dan Geringer. The headline read 'A RISING WIT' ANITA THE DJ. He described me as having a "lyrical loon laugh" and goes on to say:

Anita's mouth is just what
you always imagined it
would be. Hoped it would
be. Yearned for it to be.
Framed by large, red,
passionate lips. Peopled
by large, white, passionate
teeth. Home to a sassy,
sexually aware city wit that
cuts through your 6 A.M.
head fog quicker than
three cups of homegrown
Columbian Supremo
sweetened with honey
from bees specifically
chosen for their mental
dexterity and ability to rap
in the funky mode. After

four solid-on-the-air hours,
Anita is still cookin'. She's
sitting in her off-the-air
chair and she's wearing
tight, faded jeans and a
loose South Street Chic
tunic top and the kind of
beaded white moccasins
that you used to make in
summer camp. And her
laugh—that wild,
wraparound, totally Anita
laugh—has a life of its
own.

I signed a big contract for three years and bought a condo in the Dorchester on the twenty-third floor overlooking Rittenhouse Square. I tried to forget about Warren and it was only possible because it was so painful to think about. I gave into the early morning schedule and dealt with it. I thought that if my career went well, I would eventually start having fun again. I was making more money and buying expensive clothes. I had weekly massages and hired a woman to clean my apartment once a week. I went to every concert almost every night. The Pretenders shows always made me feel better, like I hadn't screwed up everything. Drummer Martin Chambers and I developed a platonic friendship and we spent a lot of time laughing together backstage at the shows and in the studio. Just like at WMMR, the party never stopped, especially when Soupy Sales, Bon Jovi, Mr.T., or Carole King stopped by.

Martin Chambers, the drummer for The Pretenders.

WYSP's Ken Sharp, me, Carole King, news anchor, Alice

Stockton-Rossini, and DJ Debbi Calton.

WYSP's Ed Green, Bon Jovi's Tico Torres, me, Jon Bon Jovi, Debbi Calton, record promoter David Leach, and WYSP's Mark DiDia.

Soupy Sales and I always made each other laugh.

Billboards with my face and cleavage were all over the tri-state area and I was more popular than ever. Thanks to ad man Vic Sonder and photographer Weaver Lilley I looked like how I wanted to feel. Sexy and strong. In reality I hated how I felt. I was miserable but trying so hard to hide it.

I spent a wonderful day at the "Live Aid" concert with Daryl Hall, Jack Nicholson and Graham Nash and David Letterman's bandleader, Paul Shaffer.

I barely noticed the changes going on at WYSP.

Michael Picozzi was fired and a new program director was

hired. I didn't know it at the time but the general manager,

Mel Karmazin, had hired Howard Stern to replace me and

my show. No one knew it was in the works and I couldn't

figure out why the new program director was so not into

me. I found out on August 28, the day I got fired from

WYSP. Of course it made the newspapers. Gail Shister

wrote the story.

On September 5, the headline of the TV/Radio Talk

section of the *Philadelphia Inquire*r read: THREE DJS LOSE

JOBS AT WYSP.

> They're cleaning house at
> WYSP and it's not pretty.
> Anita Gevinson, Lesley
> Patton, and Steve Sutton
> all got the boot last week.

I was quoted as saying "I don't intend to take this lying down." Actually lying down was pretty much all I did for the next couple of months. Then I got up, packed, and put my condo up for sale. I moved to the Old City section of Philadelphia and rented an apartment three doors down from Betsy Ross's house on Arch Street.

It took about a year but somehow I got hired to do a talk show. Once again I was in the newspaper. On August 4, 1986, I was back in the TV/Radio Talk section of the *Philadelphia Inquirer*. Gail Shister made me the big story. The headline read: THE PHONE RINGS AND IT'S FOR GEVINSON.

> Buckle your seatbelts,
> rocker Anita Gevinson will
> be taking over the 9 A.M. to
> 1 P.M. shift at talk station
> WCAU-AM. The audience
> response to Gevinson

during several fill in gigs at

the CBS-owned station

"was phenomenal"

according to general

manager Alan Serxner.

"We were surprised. She

was very good, even

though she hadn't done

talk radio before. We think

she'll have a wide appeal

I guess I never took the time to properly get over the break up with Warren and getting fired from WYSP. I held everything inside and finally it was just too much to handle. I stuck with the new talk show for as long as I could. I interviewed every actor and actress, author, and writer until it all started to blur together.

One day in the middle of an interview with yet another microwave cookbook author *I* was the one who had the meltdown. At the end of the show I marched into the production office and screamed at everyone. I was out of control. They called security and I was escorted to my car.

My radio career in Philly was over.

I made matters worse by taking Mel Karmazin into arbitration for breach of contract. I lost of course and packed up and moved back to L.A. I never sued for a million dollars but that didn't stop the newspaper headlines.

I was hired at a couple of stations through the years but never for a full-time shift. I still had fun on the radio, but it was never the same again. I saw Warren a couple of times but that too was never the same. We tried, but there was too much history or something. He seemed like a different person and I'm sure he felt the same about me.

As the years passed, I stopped thinking about going back to Philly and getting back together with Warren. I watched all of Warren's appearances on *Letterman* with mixed emotions. It was great to see him but it always made me sad. He did get sober and stay that way, but I never thought he looked comfortable or happy, like I remember him. I learned of his cancer diagnosis and sobbed through his final *Letterman* show. I got Warren's phone number from his friend, and owner of Artemis Records, Danny Goldberg, and called him about three months before he died. Warren didn't want me to see him but he said everything I wanted to hear him say since that day I left him in rehab. He was so kind and generous to me, trying to reassure me that I did the right thing. He told me how much he loved me and how beautiful I was and then we said goodbye.

In 2005, Nancy Palumbo, the assistant program director at WMGK reached out to me to be part of a special radio program about Warren Zevon's time in Philadelphia. A couple of months later she invited me to fill in for my friend and midday D.J. Debbi Calton on Philadelphia's classic rock station WMGK. It was a thrill and it went so well, I got to do it again in 2007 when I once again woke up too early for a morning show. My co-host, Cruze, the program director, had to listen to me bitch about the hours. I guess nothing ever changes.

It's been nine years since Warren's death and I think about him and our time together a lot. My years with Warren and my wild life on the radio were magical and I miss all that I once had. When I hear a song on the radio that takes me back to those days it makes me wish I could do it all again.

ACKNOWLEDGMENTS

Special thank you to Patrick Price, my brilliant editor, and my hero.

This would not have been possible without the help of Robin Brum, George Gruel, Maria Leonhauser, Alex Rodriguez, Scott Weiner, Nora Wells and, of course, my mother Janet, who promised me she would only look at the pictures.

Thank you also to Randy Alexander, Larry Baker, Mickie Boyer, Debbi Calton, Capri Caffe, Lynn and David Cashell, Dr. Connie Chein, Cruze, Dr. Catherine Dang, Jim Daniels, Val D'Ambrosio, Eric Davis, Terry Edwards, Danny Goldberg, Adele Greenfield, Merilee Kelly, Dr. David Kulber, Larry Magid, Drew Matusow, Harriet Mauze, Jan Moyer, Eric Molina, Meredith, Chris and Sloan Ostrow, Nancy Palumbo, Dr. Dorothy Park, Joan and Ron Porath, Chip Roberts, Blair Sabol, Carol and Bob Schwartz,

Ken Sharp, Jorge Silveira, Luca Silveira, Bobbi Silver,

Chris Stephens, Jessica Velmans, and Jordan Zevon.

PHOTO CREDITS

All photographs by Scott Weiner or from the author's private collection unless otherwise noted below.

<u>Chapter 6</u>

Photos of Warren Zevon by Phil Ceccola

<u>Chapter 9</u>

Photos of Daryl Hall and onstage at the Paradise by V.L. Gozbekian

<u>Chapter 11</u>

Photo of Roy Orbison by Ebet Roberts

Chapter 12

Photo of me and WYSP fans by Eric. R. Davis

<u>Chapter 14</u>

Photo of WYSP morning show by Susan Winters

Photo by me at Pretenders concert at Mann Music Center by Sam Cali

Photos of Martin Chambers, Carole King and Bon Jovi by Eric R. Davis

ABOUT THE AUTHOR

Anita Gevinson lives in Los Angeles, California where she continues her radio career since she is not qualified to do anything else and the phone sex industry doesn't offer adequate healthcare.